BIG RED

BIG RED

Baseball, Fatherhood, and
My Life in the Big Red Machine

Ken Griffey
With Phil Pepe

TRIUMPH
BOOKS

No part of this publication may be reproduced, stored in a retrieval system, or transmitted in any form by any means, electronic, mechanical, photocopying, or otherwise, without the prior written permission of the publisher, Triumph Books LLC, 814 North Franklin Street, Chicago, Illinois 60610.

Library of Congress Cataloging-in-Publication Data

Griffey, Ken
  Big red : baseball, fatherhood, and my life in the big red machine / Ken Griffey With Phil Pepe.
    pages cm
  ISBN 978-1-60078-544-3
  1. Griffey, Ken 2. Baseball players—United States—Biography. I. Klingner, Janette K. II. Title.
  GV865.G69A3 2014
  796.357092—dc23
  [B]
                          2014000122

This book is available in quantity at special discounts for your group or organization. For further information, contact:

   Triumph Books LLC
   814 North Franklin Street
   Chicago, Illinois 60610
   (312) 337-0747
   www.triumphbooks.com

Printed in U.S.A.

ISBN: 978-1-60078-544-3

Design by Patricia Frey

Photos courtesy of CEI Sports except where otherwise noted.

Four generations of male Griffeys have made their mark on various fields of athletic competition and received their due, so this book is dedicated to the female members of the clan:

To my beloved and courageous mother, Ruth Naomi "Ninky" Bailey Griffey, who raised six children as a single parent, provided for us, gave us discipline and love, and kept us on the straight and narrow.

To my sister, Ruby, the only girl in a maze of five male siblings.

To my daughter, Lathesia "Tee" Lockridge, who I pridefully watched blossom into a beautiful and loving woman.

To Keanna, Gabrielle, and Taryn, three lovely young women who make a granddad proud.

To my first wife, Alberta "Birdie", who did a wonderful job raising our sons, Ken Jr. and Craig, while I was off playing baseball.

And to my wife, Val, for her support, companionship, and love.

CONTENTS

FOREWORD

MY FRIENDSHIP WITH KEN GRIFFEY SENIOR DATES BACK more than four decades. In 1973, I was demoted by the Cincinnati Reds to their Triple-A affiliate in Indianapolis, Indiana. It was there that I first met Ken.

We both were young and working our way to the glorified place called the major leagues. We both had dreams of making it to baseball's highest level.

You might think that since we were both outfielders on the same team, essentially competing for the same position, that there would be some sort of rivalry between us. That definitely was not the case. We both understood that the formula for success was when opportunity meets preparation. We worked hard and smart to be prepared for the opportunity.

Ken was a left-handed hitter and thrower with outstanding running speed. He was more of a line-drive hitter who hit for a high average. He was a great athlete. It was later that I learned that in high school he not only performed well in baseball, but was a star in football, basketball, and track. He received many scholarship offers in all those sports.

When I was sent down I was angry with the world. I thought about quitting the game. Rooming with Ken became the turning point in my baseball career. We not only became good friends but *great* friends, a relationship that has endured. He helped me to enjoy the game again. He advised me not to try to be perfect; practice makes you better, not perfect. He urged me to invest the time and effort into getting better. And he assured me that the application would enhance great returns.

I discovered that Ken was a person overflowing with confidence and talent. He might tell me that he was going 5-for-5 and I would humor him and say, "Yeah, right!" And he would go out and do it. No brag, just fact. I was quickly and completely won over by Ken. It was great having a roommate with so much confidence in himself. I took my cue from him in striving always to be at my best. Consequently no manager ever had to worry about us being in shape or staying out after curfew. We were always prepared for the next game.

Ken is one of the strongest-minded individuals I have ever been around. Whatever might be going on in his life, whatever problems he might be having off the field, he never let it affect his play. I guess the word to describe him is compartmentalized. Whatever he was doing at a particular time, that's what he focused on.

Ken and I would feed off one another when we were playing. I got a lot from him just by seeing how he dealt with various situations and that helped me to grow. I learned not to let outside influences bother me.

Ken and I are a lot alike. We are both family oriented. My mom was always there for me when I was growing up and Ken's mom was always there for him. Ken has passed that along to his own kids and his grandkids. He loves his kids and grandkids and he would do anything and go anywhere for them.

Being Ken's teammate, roommate, and friend not only jump-started my baseball career, it has taught me life skills: to make adjustments in life not excuses, to be encouraging to others and not discouraging. He epitomizes what it takes to be successful in life: commitment, dedication, and not becoming complacent.

I appreciate Ken for being a positive influence in my life. Congratulations on your book, my friend.

—George Foster

INTRODUCTION

HAVING PASSED MY 40TH BIRTHDAY, I FELT FORTUNATE AND privileged when the Seattle Mariners contacted me and offered to sign me as a free agent after I had been released by the Cincinnati Reds.

I'm not going to say it wasn't about the money—it's *always* about the money—but in this case it was more than just the money.

It meant an opportunity to extend my career—I was in my 18th major league season and would be joining my fourth major league team.

It meant I could, for the time being, put off getting a "real" job.

It meant I could avoid having to "grow up" and continue to play a kid's game.

I obtained my release from the Reds on August 24, 1990, and signed with the Mariners on August 29, 1990. Two nights later, I was in the starting lineup playing left field and batting second against Storm Davis and the Kansas City Royals.

In 46 games with the Reds, I had batted only .206—the lowest average of my career by some 45 points—with one home run and eight runs batted in. But I figured the Mariners were looking at my *total* résumé—a lifetime average of .296, more than 2,000 hits, 832 RBIs, 148 home runs, three All-Star selections, and two World Series championships—and counting on me to provide a veteran presence, some stability and experience to a young, largely inexperienced team that was on the way up.

When I joined them, the Mariners had a record of 63–68 and were next to last in the seven-team American League West, 18½ games behind the Oakland Athletics. Seattle had joined the American League as an expansion team in 1977. In their 14th season in 1990, the team still had never finished with a winning record. But they were hopeful that they were about to turn the corner, because their future was in the hands of a group of promising young players.

I was the old man of the team, and the other guys never let me forget it. I was only eight years younger than the manager, Jim Lefebvre, and six years older than the team's next-oldest player, Jeffrey Leonard, a slugging outfielder, who turned 35 on September 22, finished out the season with the Mariners, was released, and never played another major league game.

Pete O'Brien (32), and Harold Reynolds, Dave Valle, and Alvin Davis (all 29), were the other "old" guys on the team, but mostly I was surrounded by kids such as the following: a promising 22-year-old left-handed-hitting first baseman named Tino Martinez; a 23-year-old glove magician at shortstop named Omar Vizquel; a 26-year-old powerful right-handed-hitting outfielder named Jay Buhner; and a couple "young" veterans in 27-year-old Edgar Martinez, an outstanding right-handed hitter, and a 26-year-old, 6'10" flame-throwing left-hander named Randy Johnson, "the Big Unit," who would go on to win 303 games, strike out 4,875 batters, pitch two no-hitters—one of them a perfect game—and win five Cy Young Awards.

But the prize gem on the team was a kid center fielder in his second major league season. As a 19-year-old rookie with only 129 minor league games and 552 minor league at-bats behind him, he had batted .264 with 16 home runs and 61 RBIs in 127 games, but he had only scratched the surface of his enormous talent. He had the promise to become one of the best players in baseball history. He stood 6'3" tall and weighed 195 pounds. He had a beautiful, picture perfect left-handed swing that caused the ball to jump off his bat and generate majestic towering home runs.

He ran like a gazelle and he made miraculous, breathtaking highlight-reel catches in center field. Best of all, he played the game with joy, flair, and boyish enthusiasm. He set a trend among young people that still is ongoing by wearing his baseball cap turned around during batting practice, and he could usually be seen with an infectious smile on his face.

I found myself playing alongside the kid in my debut as a Mariner, me in left field, he in center, me batting second, he batting third. It was as if I was there to be his mentor, his guide, and his babysitter all rolled into one.

In my first at-bat as a Mariner, I singled to center field on a 1–0 pitch. He batted next and singled to right field on an 0–1 pitch. I scored our first run on a single by Alvin Davis, and the kid scored our second run moments later.

It was as if he was playing follow the leader and saying, "Anything you can do, I can do better."

Which he could! And he did.

I was supposed to be setting an example for this kid, and here he was outdoing me at every turn. I found myself being amused by the fact that I was playing second fiddle to a kid who was only 10 months past his 20th birthday.

Hey, I was old enough to be his father.

Wait a minute! I *am* his father!

BIG RED

1

DONORA

I didn't resent that my father had left my mother and siblings and me when he did, and that was because of my mom. She raised us not to hold a grudge. The only thing I heard her say was, "That's your dad."

I STRONGLY DISAGREE WHEN PEOPLE TELL ME I WAS BORN too soon, that if I had come along a few years later I would have reaped untold riches when the prices changed and Major League Baseball players were signing long-term free-agent contracts for millions of dollars.

For the record, I first saw the light of day in Donora, Pennsylvania, on April 10, 1950, which, as it turned out, was none too soon. Had I come along two years earlier, I might not be here to tell you about a career that enabled me to earn a comfortable living and support a wonderful family by playing the game I love so much.

Let me explain. And to do that, I must first tell you something about my hometown of Donora, a borough in Pennsylvania's Washington County on the Monongahela River about 23 miles south of Pittsburgh. It's in an area known by locals as "the Valley" that is composed of Donora and nearby towns Monongahela, Monessen, and Charleroi.

At the time of my birth, Donora had about 14,000 residents, most of whom worked in the steel mills and zinc plants. It's important to know that the steel mills burned coal to fire coke ovens, melt iron ore in blast furnaces, and produce finished steel in open hearths, and that the zinc plants burned coal to smelt ore and produce zinc used for creating strong steel alloys.

The mills ran constantly, 24 hours a day, belching out foul-smelling emissions of smoke that killed the grass and turned painted homes and fences black, all of which was tolerated and accepted as part of daily living in Donora because the town's economy ran on coal. Thousands of Donora men relied on the mills for employment and to feed their families, and the mills relied on the coal for power.

The coal also powered the trains that crawled through town and heated the homes to which the hardworking, physically exhausted mill hands returned from their day's labors on bitter-cold Pennsylvania winter nights.

On Tuesday, October 26, 1948, some 17 months before I was born, Donora was hit with a devastating tragedy that would forever be known as "the Deadly Smog."

Normally, the emissions from the mills dispersed into the atmosphere and caused no immediate discernible problems— although they undoubtedly resulted in long-term health problems. This time a rare atmospheric inversion caused thick, yellowish, acrid smog composed of sulfuric acid, nitrogen dioxide, fluorine, and other poisonous gases to hover over the town for days.

Nevertheless, despite the blight, Donorans went about their normal routine, and life continued as usual. The annual Halloween parade went on as scheduled on Friday evening, October 29. The next day, the stands at Legion Field were filled as the Donora High School Dragons clashed with their archrivals the Monongahela Wildcats on a football field that was so clouded with polluted air that the fans had difficulty following the action and the players had a hard time seeing the ball.

Meanwhile back in town a local doctor was urging residents to leave the area and the town's firemen were providing whiffs of oxygen to those who couldn't, or wouldn't, leave their homes. As one fireman said, "If you could chew the air hard enough, you could swallow it."

"There never was such a fog," said another fireman. "You couldn't see your hand in front of your face, day or night. Even inside the fire station, the air was blue. I drove on the left side of the street with my head out the window, steering by scraping the curb."

All the while, the mills kept running until they finally were shut down on Sunday, October 31, Halloween. By then the local hospitals were filled with residents suffering from shortness of breath, headaches, and vomiting; a local mortuary had run out of coffins; and the streets were littered with the carcasses of pets and farm animals.

Finally, on Monday, November 1, a cool rain fell and the smog began to lift. But the damage had been done. Twenty residents of Donora had died and more than a third of its 14,000 residents were suffering from some illness. The death toll from the smog eventually reached 50, including one Lukasz Musial, the father of Donora's favorite son, the great St. Louis Cardinals seven-time National League batting champion, Stan Musial. Hardly a family in Donora was spared some hardship as a result of the smog, mine included. A year after the disaster, an elderly cousin on my father's side passed away from respiratory problems he incurred because of the smog.

Twenty-two years after the disaster, Congress passed the Clean Air Act and President Nixon signed it into law.

The Griffey clan had its roots in Shepherdstown, West Virginia, from where they migrated up to Donora, where my dad was born and raised. My father's name was Robert Joseph Griffey, but his friends called him Buddy.

My mom was named Naomi Bailey, but for some reason—I never knew why—she went by the name Ruth or by her nickname, Ninky.

My dad was an outstanding athlete at Donora High School and went to Kentucky State University in Frankfort on a football scholarship, and that's where he met my mother. She was born in Frankfort, the youngest of 11 children. She was the starting center on the women's basketball team at an all-black high school. Her family lived across from the campus of Kentucky State, and that's how she and my dad got together.

Because my dad's home was in Donora, that's where my mom and dad settled, and then the kids started to come. Jim was the oldest—his nickname was Squeeze—and he kind of took care of us younger siblings. Ron was next. He was three years younger than Squeeze. Then came Bill, Ruby (the only girl), me, and Freddy, each about a year younger than the one before.

My brother Bill had cataracts at the age of six, and they didn't know much about cataracts in those days. My mother had to take him back and forth from Donora to a hospital in Pittsburgh, 30 miles away, for treatment. Eventually he had his eye removed and a glass eye installed. My mom would have to take out the glass eye every day and clean it. We kids would watch in horror as she took Bill's glass eye out, and we'd sit there and cry.

I was born in our house on Wise Street. The name on my birth certificate is George Kenneth Griffey. I was named after my paternal grandfather. Everybody called me George, including all the kids in school. Only my brothers and sister called me Ken, because they didn't like the name George. As I got older and my friends began calling each other by nicknames, as kids like to do, they decided that my nickname should be my middle name, and the name Ken stuck.

As a boy I never knew my father. I grew up without him. When he returned to Donora after college, my dad worked in the steel mill, and when I was about two years old the mill closed and he was out of a job with a wife and six kids to feed. He decided to send us back to Kentucky to my maternal grandmother's home. His plan was to leave us in Kentucky and look for a job and then send for us after he found work. So he took us to Pittsburgh, dropped us off at the bus station, and left. We were supposed to take the bus to Kentucky, but my dad didn't give my mom enough money. So we headed back to Donora, 30 miles away, to get some more money for the bus.

When we got back to Donora, my dad was getting ready to leave. He never even told my mother he was planning to take off. She said, "You go do whatever you have to do. Don't worry about us if you feel that's the right thing to do." I didn't see him again until 14 years later, when he showed up at our door one day. I didn't even know who he was. I didn't know what he looked like. After all, I was only two when he left.

With my dad gone, my mom was left to raise six kids on the meager salary she earned at a local funeral home dressing the hair of the deceased. Needless to say, without a father and with so little money coming in, times were rough. My mom did the best she could. Between her small pay from the funeral home and collecting welfare checks, there was always enough to put food on the table and clothes on our backs, but very little for luxuries. There was not even money for Christmas presents, but one year my mom gave my brother and me an electric football game. She bought it on layaway and finally paid it off two weeks before Christmas. She hid it under her bed, but my brother and I discovered her hiding place, and when she went to work we'd take the game out from under her bed and play with it for those two weeks before Christmas. When December 25 came and Mom put the game under the tree, we had to pretend that we were surprised to get such a wonderful gift.

My mom was the rock of our family...the backbone, the stabilizer. She had to be mother and father, disciplinarian and counsel, breadwinner and caregiver. She was very influential in my career as well as my life. She kept me on the straight and narrow and was always there for me, for all of her kids. Because she never had the customary nine-to-five kind of job, she was able to adjust her work schedule, and as a result, when my brothers and I began playing sports, she went to every track meet, every football, basketball, and baseball game that we competed in. She never missed a game. There was this older man in town named Johnny Johnson—we called him "Grand Johnny"—and she paid him a dollar or two for gas or to buy himself a sandwich to drive her to our games.

My mom was strong because she had to be strong. She had it rough as a single parent of six kids, and to make matters worse, she was looked on as an outcast because she wasn't from Donora. My dad was a native and a high school sports star and was so popular and so well liked in town that when he left, the perception was that my mom was responsible for pushing Buddy Griffey—a native son and a Hall of Fame child of Donora—out of town.

I didn't resent that my father had left my mother and siblings and me when he did, and that was because of my mom. She raised us not to hold a grudge. The only thing I heard her say was, "That's your dad." From the time I started to understand this stuff, when I was 10 or 11, I never heard my mom say anything derogatory about him. She never influenced my siblings or me to think ill of my dad. My younger brother Freddie never even saw our father. I have very little knowledge of my roots, on either my dad's side or my mom's side, because my mom never talked about either of their ancestors.

Because of my mom's pleasant nature, I grew up with no resentment against my dad. Besides, I had no idea what was going on in his life when he left, and I figured he must have had his reasons.

Just about everything I know about my dad, especially his athletic prowess, I learned from Stan Musial. If it wasn't for Stan, I wouldn't have known much about my father.

After I had been with the Cincinnati Reds for a while and we went to St. Louis for games against the Cardinals, Stan Musial, who was retired by then, would come to the ballpark and seek me out. He'd sit with me and tell me things about my father. He and my dad were very close. They were teammates at Donora High and on some sandlot teams. Musial told me my dad was an outstanding athlete in three sports.

One story I heard around town (not from Musial) is that Stan and my dad were teammates on the Donora High basketball team and they made the state tournament in Pittsburgh. In his day, Musial was a top-notch basketball player, good enough to be offered a scholarship to play basketball at the University of Pittsburgh, an opportunity, perish the thought, that might have short-circuited his baseball career.

Having qualified for the state tournament, the Donora High basketball team traveled to Pittsburgh and went en masse to a hotel for their pregame meal. The Donora group consisted of a coach, a trainer, and 10 players—eight white kids and two blacks, one of whom was my dad. Presumably because of the black players, the hotel put up a screen between the players and the hotel's other diners. In protest of this overt act of discrimination, the entire Donora team, led by Musial, got up and walked out of the hotel.

I learned from talking to Musial that my dad was something of a local celebrity as a star athlete at Donora High School. In high school Musial was a highly regarded pitcher and my dad was a left-handed third baseman. Stan told me that the major league scouts would come to see him pitch, and that's when they spotted my dad, but they could not offer him a contract because he was black. Who knows if he might have become a major leaguer if he ever got the opportunity? But that was some 10 years before Jackie Robinson broke the color barrier, so my father never got the chance to sign a professional baseball contract.

All that was open to him as a baseball player was the Negro Leagues, but I never heard of him having any offers from those teams, even though Donora was only about eight miles away from Homestead, the site of the famous Homestead Grays, a powerhouse of the Negro National League with such stars as Josh Gibson, Buck Leonard, Cool Papa Bell, Oscar Charleston, Judy Johnson, and Willie Wells. I regret I never got to see the Grays play. They were disbanded in 1950, the year I was born. But I heard stories about those Negro League players from the older fellows in the projects.

One negative thing about the otherwise wonderful and historic signing of Jackie Robinson by the Brooklyn Dodgers was that it led to the demise of the Negro Leagues and cost many outstanding African American baseball players their livelihood, possibly my father included.

It's fair to say that growing up without a father was a hardship, yet I have my dad to thank for passing along the genes that gave me my athletic ability.

I saw my father again just briefly in 1975, when I was with the Cincinnati Reds and we were getting ready to play the Red Sox in the World Series. He eventually came into my life long-term years later when I was nearing the end of my career. He had moved to Cleveland, where he worked in the same building for more than 40 years as a custodian for Case Western Reserve, and he reached out to me when I was on a road trip to Cleveland with the Yankees. We maintained a relationship and would get together from time to time when I was in Cleveland in the five years I played for the Yankees.

Soon after my dad left, my mom moved us to the Highland Terrace projects. It was there that I learned to play all sports, my brothers teaching me the fundamentals. The projects featured an oval driveway that became our track for a series of competitive races. We'd form relay teams and compete against each other.

Early on I played Wiffle ball, a variety of stickball that was played with a broomstick for a bat and a perforated rubber ball thrown with great force at the hitter. That helped me learn to use my hands to generate bat speed and to react quickly to a ball coming toward me at great speeds.

I was about 10 when my older brother Jimmy got me started playing baseball. Everything I knew about baseball at the time, I learned from him. The older guys in my neighborhood used to encourage me. "You're a pretty good little player," they kept telling me. Some even said they expected me to be a big-league ballplayer someday, which made me feel good and motivated me to continue playing. Later, when I went to high school, I competed in football, basketball, and track, in addition to baseball.

My older brother Jimmy, who was an outstanding basketball player, was instrumental in fostering my love of sports. He taught me all sports and helped me learn the value of competing.

At Donora High, I was the only kid in the school to letter in four sports for four years—baseball, football, basketball, and track. In track I ran the 100, 220, and I broad-jumped and high-jumped. In football I was a running back and wide receiver on offense and a safety, defensive end, and monster on defense. Football was my best sport. I made first-team all-state in my senior year. As a receiver I broke every school record except one, most passes caught in a season.

Baseball was my weakest sport. When there was a conflict with baseball games and track meets scheduled on the same day, I'd compete in the track meet wearing my baseball uniform. I'd broad-jump 22 to 24 feet, high-jump 6'2" or 6'3", and then I'd take off my baseball pants, run the 100-yard dash, and then put my baseball pants back on and go over to the baseball field and play the game.

I set records in football and track and field at Donora High that will never be broken, because the school no longer exists. My 1969 graduating class was Donora High's last. That year the school districts of Donora and Monongahela merged to form the Ringgold School District. Donora High School and Monongahela High School closed their doors, and thereafter students from Donora and Monongahela attended Ringgold High School.

There was a great deal of despair in Donora, the feeling that you were trapped there and could not get out, that you were destined to spend your life working in the mills with no reasonable expectation of escaping.

The one way out seemed to be through sports, and many took advantage of that route. Football is king in southwestern Pennsylvania. Donora and surrounding towns produced many outstanding football players, but the area also produced stars in other sports. As a result, Donora is widely known throughout the state of Pennsylvania and beyond as "the Home of Champions," largely because it is the birthplace of one of baseball's truly great stars, Stanislaw Franciszek Musial—or Stasiu to his family, Stash to his friends, and Stan the Man to two generations of baseball fans.

Musial's baseball résumé is magnificent: a .331 lifetime batting average, seven National League batting championships, three Most Valuable Player awards, 3,630 hits (second to Ty Cobb for the most hits in baseball history when he retired, and remarkably, to emphasize his consistency, 1,815 hits at home and 1,815 hits on the road), 475 home runs, and 1,951 RBIs.

When he was named the National League's Most Valuable Player in 1948 and led the league in batting (.376), RBIs (131), and hits (230), he also hit 39 home runs and would have tied with Johnny Mize and Ralph Kiner for the league lead in homers—and won the triple crown—had he not lost a home run because of a rainout.

Musial never forgot his roots, and the town of Donora never forgot Musial. They honor him to this day with the Stan Musial Bridge that runs into town over the Monongahela River and a ballfield named for him in the town park.

While Musial stands as Donora's greatest athlete, there are others that made my little town proud.

Arnold "Pope" Galiffa: He earned 12 varsity letters at Donora High and attracted the attention of Earl "Red" Blaik, the legendary football coach at the United States Military Academy, where he won 11 varsity letters in football, baseball, and basketball. In his first year, Galiffa played behind quarterback Arnold Tucker on the last team in which the legendary Felix "Doc" Blanchard (Mr. Inside) and Glenn Davis (Mr. Outside) played for Army and finished with a 9–0–1 record.

The following season Galiffa took over as starting quarterback and remained so for three years. In four varsity seasons, Galiffa-led teams posted a record of 31–2–4 and had three undefeated seasons.

After graduation from the Point, First Lieutenant Arnold Galiffa served in the Korean War as a platoon leader in the 3rd Infantry Division and was awarded the Bronze Star. Upon discharge from the army, Galiffa played four years of professional football, two in the Canadian Football League and one each with the New York Giants and San Francisco 49ers. He died of colon cancer in 1978 and was inducted posthumously into the College Football Hall of Fame five years later.

"Deacon" Dan Towler: A bruising running back for the Los Angeles Rams from 1950 to 1955, Towler was a four-time Pro Bowler, the Most Valuable Player in the 1951 Pro Bowl, a member of the Rams' 1951 NFL championship team and the NFL's leading rusher in 1952. After retiring from football, he was named pastor of the Lincoln Avenue Methodist Church in Pasadena, California, was a Chaplain at California State University at Los Angeles, and became president of the Los Angeles County Board of Education. He passed away in 2001.

Ulice Payne: In 2002 he became the first African American CEO of a major league team when he headed up the Milwaukee Brewers. He also was a member of the 1977 NCAA basketball champion Marquette Warriors, coached by Al McGuire. Drafted by the Detroit Pistons, he was cut before he played a game in the NBA. Instead he went back to college and earned a law degree from Marquette.

Bernie Galiffa: My high school quarterback, and Arnold Galiffa's nephew, Bernie made a name for himself as a three-year starter at the University of West Virginia. It was said about Bernie that he was a gunslinger who never saw a forward pass he didn't like. Playing in a long-ago era (1970–72) before football became the passing game it is today, Galiffa put up impressive numbers and set a lot of school records as a passer. In three seasons he completed 310 passes for 4,426 yards and 28 touchdowns.

Lee Sala: A leading middleweight contender in the 1940s and 1950s, Sala had a career record of 76–7 with 48 knockouts, including a winning streak of 47 fights. He fought many of the top contenders of his day, including former middleweight champion Bobo Olson.

Ken Griffey Jr.: Junior was born in Donora (he shares a birthday, November 21, with Stan Musial) but left when we moved to Cincinnati when he was six. With 630 home runs (sixth all-time), 1,836 RBIs (15th all-time), and 2,781 hits (49th all-time), he's a cinch to be voted into the National Baseball Hall of Fame, and on the first ballot, as soon as he is eligible. On that happy day, he will join another Donora native, Stan Musial, in Cooperstown's hallowed halls. How many towns as small as Donora can boast of having two native sons in the National Baseball Hall of Fame?

While they are not Donora natives, Joe Montana, considered by many the greatest quarterback in NFL history, is from New Eagle, Pennsylvania, and went to Ringgold High School, and longtime Minnesota Vikings kicker Fred Cox was born in Monongahela and attended Monongahela High School.

Others from the area include the great Johnny Unitas; Pro Bowler, Hall of Fame tight end, and former coach Mike Ditka; Hall of Famer and former Heisman Trophy running back Tony Dorsett; and Darrelle Revis, all from Aliquippa High School; former Buffalo Bills quarterback Jim Kelly from East Brady High School; and "Broadway" Joe Namath from Beaver Falls.

You may have noticed the rather liberal mixture of both white and black athletes that have come out of Donora and the surrounding area. We were a small town—our high school had only 500 students and more than half were girls—so our sports teams were a mixture of whites and blacks from Little League up through high school.

We had our differences between neighbors and teammates, but I don't recall any of it being racially motivated. I had as many white friends as black friends and really didn't experience racism when I was growing up. I didn't learn anything about racism in Donora. That came later.

2
DECISION

On its final approach to Tri-State Airport, the plane collided with the tops of trees on a hillside 5,543 feet west of Runway 12, causing the plane to plummet to the ground nose-first and burst into flames, the charred wreckage coming to a stop 4,219 feet from the runway.

THE YEAR WAS 1969. I HAD JUST TURNED 19 YEARS OLD, AND I was about to graduate from Donora High School. I had come to a crossroads in my young life; I had an important decision to make. What was I going to do with the rest of my life...or at least with the next few years?

I didn't have a whole lot of options. One, which didn't appeal to me a bit, was to get a job in order to help my mom support our family. It's not that I had any aversion to work—since I was about 11 or 12 I had worked at a variety of part-time jobs to help out with finances at home—but I didn't want to end up spending my life working in the mills. I also had this burning desire to continue with athletics in some form.

I had had a very good senior year in football, made all-state, and attracted enough attention to get a few offers from colleges. I was even getting the hustle from people I knew. Bernie Galiffa had signed a letter of intent to play football at the University of West Virginia, and my cousin Larry Nelson had been recruited to play football at Marshall University in Huntington, West Virginia. The two schools were close to each other and played one another every season, so I went to the game when I was a senior in high school to see my two good friends play, and both Bernie and Larry tried to recruit me. So there was this tug-of-war going on between two of my best friends, pulling me in different directions, each telling me I would have no problem playing football at that level.

Larry had told the coaches at Marshall that I was a wide receiver, and Marshall needed a wide receiver. Bernie wanted me to go to the University of West Virginia to become his go-to receiver in college just as I had been in high school.

I found the idea of college, and especially playing college football, very appealing. But there was a problem. Even if I could get a free ride to play college football, where my tuition—and maybe even my room and board and books—would be covered, there still would be expenses my family could not afford.

My mom, who had been an outstanding basketball player as a girl back in Frankfort, Kentucky, was always supportive of my athletics while I was in high school, but once I graduated she made it clear the time had come for me to contribute to the household finances. Sadly, I came to the realization that college was out of the question and I had to turn to something that would provide me with an income that could help my mom.

Had I been able to go to college, I'm fairly certain I would have chosen Marshall, because of Larry Nelson. He was my cousin and we were very close, and that gave Marshall a slight edge over West Virginia. But once again fate intervened in my life in a most meaningful way just as it had two decades earlier when I narrowly missed being around during the notorious Donora Smog disaster.

Had I gone to Marshall, I would have been a freshman during the 1969 football season. Perhaps I would have been able to make the traveling team as a freshman, perhaps not. But I'm fairly certain I would have been on the team in my sophomore season, 1970, possibly even a starter. And as such I would have traveled with the Marshall Thundering Herd to play at East Carolina on November 14, 1970.

College football aficionados will easily recognize the date. It was the final game of a disappointing season for Marshall, which had lost five of its first eight games. For the first time all season, the Thundering Herd football team would be flying to a game away from home (all other opponents' campuses were close enough for Marshall to travel by bus).

The game against the East Carolina Pirates at Ficklen Memorial Stadium in Greenville, North Carolina, was another disappointment for Marshall, an excruciating 17–14 defeat completing a 3–6 season and assuring that the plane ride home would be somber.

Shortly after 6:00 PM Southern Airways Flight 932, a Douglas DC-9 charter, left Stallings Field in Kinston, North Carolina, for the return trip to Huntington Tri-State Airport/Milton J. Ferguson Field in Ceredo, West Virginia. At 7:23 PM, as the charter was nearing its destination, air-traffic controllers informed the crew that there was "rain, fog, and a ragged ceiling" at the airport, making landing more difficult but not impossible, and instructed them to descend to 5,000 feet. At 7:34 PM Southern Airways Flight 932 was given clearance to land.

On its final approach to Tri-State Airport, the plane collided with the tops of trees on a hillside 5,543 feet west of Runway 12, causing the plane to plummet to the ground nose-first and burst into flames, the charred wreckage coming to a stop 4,219 feet from the runway. There were no survivors. All 75 passengers on board perished, including 37 members of the Marshall University Thundering Herd football team, eight members of the coaching staff, 25 boosters—many of whom were prominent Huntington citizens—and five flight crew members. It was the deadliest sports-related tragedy in United States history. (The story of the tragedy and how Marshall University rebounded from the disaster was documented in the 2007 feature film *We Are Marshall*, starring Matthew McConaughey).

I have every reason to believe that had I gone to Marshall, I would have been on that plane.

I had recently returned home after my second professional season in Sioux Falls and I learned of the crash from my uncle, my cousin Larry Nelson's father. My first thought upon hearing this horrific news was not that I might have been on that airplane if I had gone as planned to play football at Marshall. My first thought was about my cousin.

"What about Larry?" I asked my uncle.

It was then that I learned how fate had intervened, that Larry was supposed to be on the plane but had gotten into a confrontation with one of the coaches and had been suspended for one game. It happened to be the game against East Carolina. After that, Larry's life just spun out of control. He got hooked on drugs and went slowly downhill.

I'm not a psychiatrist, but I have read enough about such things that I believe Larry's problems came about because of a sense of guilt over not being on that plane. It's called survivor's guilt. People in that sort of situation find themselves asking "Why not me? Why was I spared?" So many of Larry's teammates and friends died in that crash but he survived, and that must have haunted him. The drugs were likely his way of escaping from the reality and assuaging his guilt.

So flash back to 1969. I was 19 years old, about to graduate from high school, and at a loss as to what to do with my life. My mom needed me to contribute financially to the household, and I had no college, no money, no job, and no prospects. But I had Elmer Gray.

At the time Elmer was covering the Valley as a major league scout for the Cincinnati Reds (later, when Marge Schott bought the Reds, Elmer quit and went to work for the Pittsburgh Pirates, where he went on to have an outstanding career as a scout and then as scouting director).

Elmer also moonlighted as a high school basketball and football official in our area. He had never seen me play baseball, but he had worked Donora High's basketball and football games and was impressed by my speed and athleticism.

In high school my reputation was in football and basketball, but little did I know that during my high school days—in addition to

Gray, the Reds scout—a Pirates scout by the name of Joe Consoli had been keeping an eye on me for four years.

I had only two tryouts with the Reds, but I had tryouts galore with the Pirates from ninth grade to my senior year in high school. In my senior year, Consoli invited me to attend a Pirates tryout camp in Johnstown, PA. There were 106 kids at the camp, and Consoli split us up into sections. He had us run a 60-yard dash. I remember Consoli taking a dollar bill out of his pocket and putting it on the finish line of the 60 and saying, "This will be the first money you will earn in baseball." I outran everybody in camp. I ran a 6.1 60 and picked up Consoli's dollar bill and put it in my pocket.

Consoli told people I couldn't hit, which he probably also told the Pirates, because they never drafted me.

Meanwhile Elmer Gray had me come to two Reds tryouts in Fayette City, PA. They brought in George "Doc" Medich to pitch to me. Medich was a big-time pitching prospect from Hopewell High School in Aliquippa, PA (the same school as Tony Dorsett) and then at the University of Pittsburgh. Medich went on to pitch for 11 major league seasons with the Yankees, Pirates, and five other major league teams.

I hit a couple of balls out against him, and the next day they had a simulated game and I faced Medich again and hit another home run off him. Then they had me run a 60-yard dash, and I ran it in 6.2 or somewhere near there. Elmer Gray asked me, "If we draft you, will you sign?"

The Reds selected me in the 29th round of the 1969 MLB June Amateur Draft. I was the 682nd player taken, just behind Stanley Babieracki, a left-handed pitcher from St. John's University who was selected by the Atlanta Braves but never pitched above class AA, and just ahead of Ken Kravec, a left-handed pitcher chosen by the Cleveland Indians who pitched eight seasons for the White Sox and Cubs with a record of 43–56.

To put things in perspective, the No. 1 pick in the country in that draft was Jeff Burroughs, who had a long (16 seasons) and productive (240 home runs, 882 RBIs) career with Washington, Texas, Atlanta, Seattle, Oakland, and Toronto.

Also drafted that year were Don Gullett and Rawly Eastwick, who later became my teammates with the Reds, and J.R. Richard, Gorman Thomas, Lee Lacy, Hall of Famer Bert Blyleven, Bucky Dent, Duane Kuiper, and John Stearns.

Why did I fall so low in the draft? For one thing, the weather in Donora in the spring is so bad, we rarely played more than four or five games a season, so I didn't have much of a chance to make an impression on the scouts, and I wasn't a very highly regarded baseball player in high school. For another, it was assumed that I was going to sign a letter of intent to play football in college.

In fact, a lot of folks in Donora were surprised and—since that was and still is football country—disappointed when I chose baseball over football. What the people of Donora didn't consider, and the major league scouts had no way of knowing, was that I was forced into signing a professional baseball contract because I needed the money.

Because my reputation back home was as a football player and not a baseball player, I had my doubters who thought I was making a mistake in not pursuing football. The only two I remember who believed that I could play baseball on the next level were my friends Joe Perrotta and Ed Gray (no relation to Elmer Gray).

Joe Perrotta especially encouraged me, supported me, looked after me, and helped me in so many ways. He took care of me when I was in the army reserves. If I didn't have a ride, Joe would drive me to the meetings—which were near Cumberland, Maryland— drop me off, and then go all the way to his reserve meeting near Wheeling, West Virginia. That is how dedicated a friend Joe was. When I was playing Double A ball at Three Rivers in Canada, Joe drove on vacation all the way from Donora to Three Rivers and stayed a whole week just to watch me play. We were friends as kids, and we stayed friends. We even sponsored an annual big charity golf tournament together in Donora.

Ed Gray was active in Donora in Little League baseball and youth football. When I was 16, he put me to work for him with the Donora Youth Corps and always encouraged and supported me through my early days as a professional.

Being drafted by a major league team was not the big deal then as it has become today. The draft wasn't shown on television, it wasn't held in public, and teams didn't have press conferences for their picks (maybe for the No. 1 pick but certainly not for their 29th pick).

The Reds never even telephoned me to tell me they had drafted me. I found out when they sent me a letter. When I got the letter, I told my mom, "Hey, Mom, I've just been drafted."

"Oh, no," she said. "You got to go in the army?"

My signing "bonus" was a brand-new jockstrap and a pair of sanitary socks, no kidding. I would be paid $500 a month. After paying for room and board, reimbursing welfare with monthly payments, and sending money to my mom, there wasn't much left of that $500.

But at least it was a start, and I was on my way.

3

Pro

"Gentlemen, the name of the game is baseball, and if any of you SOBs misses a sign or a bag, it will cost you $25 every time until you get it right."

IT WAS ALL HAPPENING SO FAST. I WAS DRAFTED BY THE Cincinnati Reds on Thursday, June 5, 1969, and a couple days later I was headed to Greater Pittsburgh Airport for another first, my first airplane flight. It took me to Tampa, Florida, at the time the site of the Reds' spring-training complex.

In Tampa I was checked into the antiquated and historic Hillsboro Hotel, where I stayed for the next two weeks while going through training at Al Lopez Field on Dale Mabry Highway, which would be my spring-training "home" for the next decade.

All the players in camp at the time would make up the rosters of the Reds' two entry-level teams. There was the Reds team in the Gulf Coast Rookie League, a short-season league based in Florida with seven teams representing the Reds, Montreal Expos, Cleveland Indians, Pittsburgh Pirates, Chicago White Sox, Minnesota Twins, and St. Louis Cardinals, and then there was the Sioux Falls Packers of the short-season Class A Northern League, which was considered one step up from Bradenton. All the players in camp were either just out of the recent amateur draft, signed as free agents, or had played the previous year at Bradenton. I was assigned to the Gulf Coast League team.

In those two weeks, we went through instruction, infield, and batting practice, and to break up the monotony we'd play games, Bradenton against Sioux Falls. I played for Bradenton, and Don Gullett and Ross Grimsley—a couple of nasty, hard-throwing left-handers—pitched for Sioux Falls. Are you kidding? I couldn't hit them with a paddle. I figured the coaches would see me flailing away at those two and that would be the end of my professional baseball career. Instead, when the two weeks were up, I was on my way to Bradenton as planned.

Three teams in the league were based in Bradenton, a town on Florida's Gulf Coast about 40 miles south of Tampa. The other teams were based in Sarasota. We were to play a 54-game schedule with all games at the Pirates spring-training field in Bradenton or the White Sox spring-training field in Sarasota, about 13 miles south of Bradenton.

On the morning we were to break camp in Tampa and take off for Bradenton, we assembled in a meeting room at the hotel and one player after another was called on, and he mentioned the names of three teammates who would be his roommates in Bradenton. After a while I noticed that only three players had not been assigned a room or a roommate, and I was one of the three. Like me, the other two were black. It was obvious that we had no choice; it had been decided for us that we three would room together.

I learned later that the night before, the white players had been informed that they should get together to decide who they wanted as roommates and that they would be called on the next morning to reveal the names of their bunkmates. The black players were never so informed.

My two roommates were Clarence Cooper and Willis Ham. Cooper (we called him Petey) was a left-handed pitcher who had been drafted by the Reds in the fifth round of the 1969 Amateur Draft. Petey was from Frederick, Maryland, where he played baseball and football and was the quarterback on the high school team that starred the great Minnesota Vikings running back Chuck Foreman.

Ham was from Charleston, South Carolina, and had been an outstanding football star at South Carolina State University, where he used his unbelievable speed to lead the nation in punt returns. He signed with the Reds as an undrafted free agent. Willis later went on to a wonderful career in college athletics as athletic director at his alma mater for 10 years. He was elected to the National Association of Collegiate Directors of Athletics Hall of Fame in 2008.

Naturally, the three of us hit it off and became not only roommates but close friends, practically inseparable in that first year. We very much needed each other in those days. Not only was I away from home for the first time in my life, I was encountering situations I had never faced before and never really knew existed.

In 1969 the Civil Rights Act had been in force for five years, but somehow the news hadn't seemed to arrive in Bradenton, which was still very much considered the Deep South, with many of the old prejudices. For the first time in my life, I saw segregated drinking fountains, movie theaters, and restaurants.

One night Petey, Willis, and I walked to a local grocery store in downtown Bradenton to get some provisions, and this big, black Cadillac came up on us, right onto the sidewalk, and almost hit us. I thought the guy was drunk or sick or something, but the next thing we knew here came the Cadillac again.

"Let's get out of here," Willis said. "That car is trying to hit us."

That was the last time we even went downtown. I was stunned, because I didn't know what was happening. I just figured, *This man's crazy. What's his problem?* That's how naïve I was about such things back then.

I had never experienced anything like that, but Willis had. I was 19 at the time and Petey was 18, but Willis was the "old man" of our group, a mature 22-year-old and a college graduate. A year before, as a junior at South Carolina State, he was on campus when three of his friends were killed on the grounds of their college by South Carolina Highway Patrol officers. The incident became known as the Orangeburg Massacre. It occurred the same year Dr. Martin Luther King Jr. was assassinated and two years before the shootings at Jackson State University and Kent State University.

Because Willis had experienced racial bias firsthand, Petey and I leaned on him to make some sense out of the madness.

At Bradenton, I came under the influence of George Scherger, our manager and one of the great baseball characters, who was known affectionately as "Sugar Bear." George spent almost a half century in baseball, most of it in the minor leagues as a player, coach, and manager. He got his big break when Sparky Anderson became manager of the Reds in 1970. Scherger had managed Sparky in the minor leagues, and Sparky made him his first-base coach. Scherger was Sparky's right-hand man during his nine years as Reds manager. Pete Rose once called Scherger "the greatest baseball mind in the world."

That great baseball mind stood in the locker room at Bradenton's McKechnie Field, in front of a group of teenagers and 20-somethings getting ready to begin their professional baseball careers. "Gentlemen," he said, "the name of the game is baseball, and if any of you SOBs misses a sign or a bag, it will cost you $25 every time until you get it right."

I immediately got the message. I was already in a hole financially with my living expenses, having to repay welfare, and sending money home to my mom and to my girlfriend (who was pregnant with our first child). I knew I couldn't afford to also pay a fine of $25. So I made it my business to make sure I didn't miss any signs or bases. I had no choice. I had to succeed in baseball because I needed the money, so I worked my butt off.

Baseball in Bradenton was a grind. We'd be in uniform at 8:00 in the morning and go through drills and instructions, batting and fielding practice most of the day, and then we'd play a doubleheader that night. It was exhausting, but we were learning and we were improving.

Back in the day there were no rovers (instructors roving through the minor league affiliates) and no coaches. You'd have a manager who manned the third-base coach's box when the team was at bat, and a pitching coach. If you were lucky you might have a manager who knew something about hitting, but that was rare. Mostly what you learned you had to learn on your own, and it was well known that if you didn't hit you were gone.

When I was young, my idol was Lou Brock, a left-handed hitter like me. I even tried to hit like him, mimicking his closed stance. Back then I couldn't hit a slider. I had never seen a slider in high school, but when I got to pro ball it seemed to me all they threw were sliders. I had to make an adjustment quickly, but there was nobody to help me. I was left to figure things out for myself. I opened my stance and squared up, and that enabled me to hit the slider. From that day forward, I started understanding that in order to survive, you had to make adjustments from pitcher to pitcher and from pitch to pitch, and you had to make the adjustments quickly, on the fly; you couldn't wait to do it two or three days down the road. By then you might be 0-for-20 and on your way home.

It wasn't rocket science. I understood that each pitcher has a different delivery and release point. I learned how to pick up the ball, and that's how I improved as a hitter.

There was no such thing as waiting until you got to the big leagues to learn. That's what the minor leagues were for. I was fortunate that in the minors I had guys that taught fundamentals— hit the cutoff man, know when to run, know when not to run, know where to go with the ball, understand what the situations are. That's what we were taught in the minor leagues. When we got to the big leagues, Sparky Anderson wasn't going to teach us how to play the game. If you missed the cutoff man or threw to the wrong base, you weren't going to play. By the time we got to the big leagues, our job was to know what we had to do in all situations.

I had a pretty good first year as a professional. I played in 49 of our 54 games and batted .281, which was 18th-best in the league. I led the league in doubles with 11, hit one triple, one home run, drove in 12 runs, and was second in the league with 11 stolen bases.

I returned home to Donora feeling pretty good about myself. On September 4 my girlfriend, Birdie, and I eloped. We drove in her car, just the two of us, all the way from Donora to Winchester, Virginia, to get married because that was the closest place we could find where we could get married before we were 21. My mother had to sign a paper, her mother had to sign a paper; her dad didn't even know we were getting married.

Seven weeks later, on November 21, Birdie gave birth to a baby boy. We named him George Kenneth Griffey Jr., but nobody called him George, either. He was either Ken or Junior.

I don't like to make excuses, but I'm going to make the case that circumstances beyond my control made it difficult for me to succeed in my second year as a professional.

The military draft was on in 1970, and I was fair game to be called, so the Reds arranged for me to join the army reserves and fulfill my military obligation by doing my six months of active duty and then following up with summer camp, weekend meetings, and monthly meetings. That would allow me to continue uninterrupted with my baseball career, but there was a price to pay.

At the same time, for a period of five years while I was in the minor leagues, I had to avoid the authorities or I could have been thrown into jail as a "deadbeat dad." Let me explain why.

Every year while I was in the minor leagues, I returned home when the season ended, and I had no money coming in. None! I knew I had to get a job to support my family, but it wasn't like I was a college kid who was home for the summer and had a job waiting for him. I had to go out and hustle for a job. I went to every place in the Monongahela Valley—the Mesta Mining Company, Duquesne Mills, Christy Park Steel Mill,—to hunt for a job. I'd fill out an application and return home hoping I got a call that I had been hired.

Eventually, I wound up with a variety of odd jobs. I worked at the Christy Park Steel Mill in McKeesport on garbage detail. My job was to collect the waste from the mill in a small can and dump it into a larger can. That's all I did every day, for eight hours, five days a week. After I was there a while they trained me on the line. I would take little pins and stick them into holes in preparation for making bombs for Vietnam.

The people at work knew I was a professional baseball player, but they didn't seem to care. They didn't like the idea that I was playing baseball. I was supposed to play football, so I was not treated as a celebrity, and I didn't get any preferential treatment.

Until I got a job, I still had to feed my family. But I had no money and no choice except to have my wife apply for welfare. I accompanied her to the welfare office, where the caseworker had her fill out papers in which she was to state why she had no money. He advised her to say that she was making her claim based on the fact that her husband was a deadbeat dad, which is a felony. Later I was told by the caseworker that if the police saw me on the street, they could haul me off to jail for non-support.

"But don't worry," he said. "The papers are not going to leave my desk. As soon as you get a job, come back and tell me, and the papers will disappear."

About two weeks later, the caseworker gave my wife a check and food stamps, and I became a "fugitive."

We followed the same program every year for five or six years until I got to the big leagues and was making the major league minimum (in 1973 the major league minimum salary was $15,000; in 1963 it had been $6,000, so in 10 years the minimum salary had increased by $9,000) and I was able to support my family and to begin repaying the government for the welfare checks.

On January 1, 1970, I left my wife and my baby boy in Donora, and on a day as cold as a bigot's heart, I took a bus to the Pittsburgh

Airport and boarded a plane for Fort Leonard Wood, Missouri, where I spent the next five and a half months playing soldier. It made getting ready for the baseball season difficult and, I firmly believe, was part of the reason I had such a horrible season.

Things had been going pretty well up to that point. My success at Bradenton made me think that this baseball stuff wasn't so tough, after all. I figured I was on the fast track to Cincinnati, but I soon got my comeuppance and a large dose of baseball reality and personal humility. For the 1970 season, the Reds moved me up to Sioux Falls, which turned out to be a horror show for me on several levels.

To begin with, Sioux Falls, South Dakota, in the late '60s and early '70s wasn't the most progressive, liberal, and tolerant city in the union. It also had something of a pigment problem. There were no black people in Sioux Falls, and we had three black kids on the team—me and two Southern Californians, Chris Jones, an outfielder who was 21 and was actually a schoolteacher, and a big high school kid named Rex Jackson, a right-handed pitcher who was only 17. He was a second-round draft pick who threw hard. He could have been a football player. He was big, and he kind of looked like Jim Brown.

The first nine days the team was at home, the three of us were forced to live for a time in the street. The club only provided us with three days in a hotel. After that you were on your own. Chris knew this guy who had the key to a dorm room at Augustana College, so we borrowed the key and sneaked into the dorm at night to sleep. But we had to vacate the room every morning at 6:00 because the custodian was coming to clean the rooms, and that's when we went on the street and tried to find someplace to finish our night's sleep.

Meanwhile my wife was back home in Donora with my baby boy and feeling lonely. Without telling me, she decided to pack up Junior and come to Sioux Falls. When I learned of her plans, I tried reaching her to tell her not to come, because I was getting ready to go on a nine-day road trip and I didn't have a place for them to live. But welfare had already paid for her flight to Sioux Falls, South Dakota, and she was on the plane.

What was I going to do when they got there? I couldn't take them to the dorm. I couldn't have them sleep in the street. I went back to the hotel and got a room for $10 a night.

"Can you afford to have your family stay here for nine days?" the hotel owner asked.

I told him it didn't matter, because even if I could not afford it, there was no way I was leaving my wife and baby alone while I went on a nine-day road trip. My wife was the only black woman in the whole city of Sioux Falls. I was planning to have my wife and Junior stay until the day before I left on the road trip, and then I'd take them back to Donora.

"I have a nephew in real estate," the hotel owner said. "I'll call him and see if he can find you a place to live."

The day before I was to take my family back home, the hotel owner said his nephew had found me a furnished one-bedroom apartment that would cost me $60 a month.

That should have been the end of my troubles. It wasn't. I should have continued on my fast track to Cincinnati. I didn't. I had a terrible year. My batting average dropped off to .244, and I hit two home runs and drove in 24 runs—not much better than I had done at Bradenton. I was worried about leaving my family alone every night, because there were things going on in Sioux Falls. Police in town were hunting a rapist. I still had to go on road trips and leave my wife and baby alone, and I worried about them because they stood out in Sioux Falls like a sore thumb. It was hard to concentrate on playing baseball.

I had hit bottom. It forced me to reach down into my soul and remember something my mother had told me before I went off to play in my first year as a professional. My mom and my oldest brother Jim had been my strongest influences. When I was young, my mom said, "Once you get between the white lines, there's nobody that's better than you."

I kept that thought with me throughout my career, and that's the way I played. I never thought anybody—Pete Rose, Joe Morgan, Johnny Bench...anybody—was better than me. I was going to play my game, but I was going to play just as hard as anybody else, if not harder. And that was my philosophy and my motivation for my entire career.

I constantly reminded myself that I had nothing to lose but everything to gain because I didn't have a college education and had a family to support. If I didn't play very well and didn't do the things I needed to do in order to get to the big leagues, I'd have been a steel-mill worker. I worked in the steel mills during the off-season early in my career, and I decided that was one thing I did not want to do.

My way of thinking was "mentally strong on both sides." I came to know exactly how the front office operated in baseball, how they were going to react, what they were thinking about players, and how I needed to survive. I knew that as a player I had to play better than anybody. I could not afford a mental letdown. I told myself that the only way I was going to impress the front office and the only way I was going to survive was by playing hard every day in games and working hard every day in practice.

I understood that I was a commodity. In other words, if you don't produce, they'll get rid of you. That's how I played, and that's what I imparted to Junior when his time came.

After completing my military obligation with five and a half months of active duty, I was ready to dive headlong into baseball and commit myself to being the best player I could be and to reach my ultimate goal of making it in the major leagues.

I went to spring training with the Tampa Tarpons in the high Class A Florida State League in 1971, a pretty big jump for someone who had hit only .244 in a short-season Single A league the year before. Maybe the Reds were purposely forcing me, expecting me to fail so they could release me. I kept expecting the ax to fall. The only thing that saved me was that a few guys got hurt and I was the only left-handed hitting outfielder they had left.

At Tampa, one of my teammates was Dan Driessen, who became one of my best friends. Dan, who was a year younger than me, was from South Carolina. Like me he was a left-handed hitter, but he played first base and third base, so we were not competing for the same job and therefore were no threat to one another. Instead, we became friendly rivals, each of us trying to outdo the other, pushing each other, all to the good of both of us and the team.

My .342 average at Tampa was the highest in the Florida State League, but I didn't have enough at-bats to qualify for the league's batting title. Nevertheless, it was 98 points higher than I had hit the year before at Sioux Falls. Driessen was fourth in the league at .327, so we formed a pretty good one-two punch for the Tarpons. I was also second in the league with 11 triples and seventh in stolen bases, with 25 in 88 games.

My time in Tampa was cut short when the Reds moved me up in the final two weeks of the season to the Class AA Eastern League, where I was to join a new team in a new league in a new country, the Three Rivers Eagles—or Trois-Rivieres Aigles, as they were known in Quebec—who were in the playoffs.

At Three Rivers I got into nine games and had 13 hits in 32 at-bats, a batting average of .406, which probably impressed the Reds, because they assigned me back to Three Rivers for the 1972 season. I played in 128 games, hit 21 doubles, three triples, and for the first time showed some power with 14 home runs. I also knocked in 52 runs, was fourth in the league with 31 stolen bases, and fourth in hitting with a .318 average. This time my buddy Driessen outhit me and finished one notch above me, third in the league at .322.

Dan and I were both moved up to the Indianapolis Indians in the Class AAA American Association, the highest team in the Cincinnati Reds farm system and the last rung on the ladder up to the big club.

At Indianapolis I had another good season. I was seventh in the league in hitting, with a .327 average, and I led the league in stolen bases with 43. I also had 18 doubles, five triples, 10 homers, and 58 RBIs in 107 games. Driessen, however, was having a monster year, batting .409 with six home runs and 46 RBIs in 47 games in June when the Reds called him up to the majors.

My promotion came about 10 weeks later.

REDS

We found the entrance to the home-team clubhouse, and I was directed to my locker, in which was hanging a fresh, clean white uniform with the number 30 on the back.

MIDWAY THROUGH THE 1973 SEASON, I WAS ON A TRIP TO Des Moines, Iowa, with the Indianapolis Indians. We had a night game, so to kill time I went to a downtown movie theater to see *Hercules Unchained*, a fantasy action flick starring Steve Reeves. I was enjoying the movie when I heard somebody shout, "Is Ken Griffey here?"

It turned out it was the manager of the theater. Fortunately, I had mentioned to some of my teammates that I was going to the movies, and apparently there was only one movie house in downtown Des Moines, so they tracked me down.

I walked up to the theater manager and identified myself.

"You have to go back to the hotel," he said. "Your manager wants to talk to you."

Vern Rapp, my Indianapolis manager, was waiting for me at the hotel with news for Will McEnaney, Ed Armbrister, and me. It was the sort of news every minor league player likes to hear and every minor league manager likes to deliver: "You're all being sent up to the big leagues."

Your immediate reaction when you hear those words is joy, vindication, and satisfaction for having reached your goal (it took almost five years; I wasn't exactly an overnight sensation).

Next, your mind becomes a computer, cataloging all the things you have to do before you depart—airplane reservations (the Reds traveling secretary will take care of that), find a place to live in Cincinnati (the club will make arrangements), gather up your equipment (bats, gloves, spiked shoes), pack your clothes—and you try to think what players on the Reds you know. The only one there that I had any kind of relationship with was my buddy Dan Driessen.

There were a few others I knew from being in spring training with the Reds, but I wasn't really close to any of them.

At the time, the Reds were in a resurgence. Led by a group of outstanding young players, they had become one of the powers of the National League.

Baseball's oldest professional team, the Reds had gone through a down period in the 1960s. They had won the pennant in 1961 under manager Fred Hutchinson, who kept them in contention for the next two years. But Hutch contracted cancer and died on November 12, 1964, and with him gone, the team suffered.

Without Hutchinson, the Reds dropped to fourth place in 1965. After the season, they traded Frank Robinson, their best player, to the Baltimore Orioles, claiming that Robinson was getting old (he had turned 30 four months earlier) and on the decline.

In six seasons with the Orioles, "Old Man" Robinson made the All-Star team five times, won a Most Valuable Player award, hit more than .300 four times, blasted 179 home runs, drove in 545 runs, and helped the Orioles win four American League pennants and two World Series.

Meanwhile, in their first three years without "Old Man" Robinson, the Reds plummeted to seventh place, fourth place, and fourth place again. They seemed to turn things around under Dave Bristol, their third manager since Hutchinson, who brought them in third in 1969.

But management apparently was dissatisfied with Bristol, so when the 1970 season began, the Reds had a new manager. His name was George Lee Anderson, but he was known as "Sparky," if he was known at all. By his own admission, Sparky was "a nobody."

As a player, his major league career consisted of one season as a second baseman for the 1959 Philadelphia Phillies in which he batted a robust .218, hit no home runs, drove in 34 runs, and had 104 hits, 92 of them singles. Needless to say, the Phillies did not invite him back in 1960. Instead, Anderson began a much-traveled minor league career as a manager, winning four championships in four years with four different teams in four different leagues. As his reward, he was asked by manager Preston Gomez to be a coach for the expansion San Diego Padres in 1969, their first season. Sparky quickly accepted.

The following year, California Angels manager Lefty Phillips, Sparky's buddy, mentor, and the man who signed him to his first professional contract, asked Anderson to join his coaching staff. Again Sparky quickly agreed. But before he could even put on an Angels uniform, Cincinnati general manager Bob Howsam, for whom Sparky had worked in the minor leagues, called and offered him the job of manager of the Reds. Naturally, Sparky jumped at the chance. At age 36 he became the youngest manager in the major leagues.

The news that Sparky Anderson was hired to be the new manager of the Reds hit the city of Cincinnati like a thunderbolt. Not only was Anderson a complete unknown with no résumé as a major league player and no track record as a manager in the major leagues, he was replacing the wildly popular Dave Bristol. Had Bob Howsam taken leave of his senses? The headline in one Cincinnati paper the next day simply read: SPARKY WHO?

Anderson inherited a team that included 28-year-old right fielder Pete Rose and 27-year-old third baseman Tony Perez, two players in the prime of their careers, but only one pitcher (Jim Merritt) who had won more than 12 games, plus a handful of other pitchers: 33-year-old Al Jackson, 34-year-old Pedro Ramos, and 35-year-old Camilo Pascual, who Sparky knew had to be replaced.

Anderson's mission was to weed out the older players and make the team younger. Toward that end, one of his first decisions was to anoint 21-year-old Venezuelan rookie Dave Concepcion his starting shortstop. Davey was so gifted that he significantly improved the team's defense and was a huge benefit to the pitching staff. Merritt went from 17 wins in 1969 to 21 in 1970; 22-year-old Gary Nolan went from eight wins to 18; and Wayne Granger and Clay Carroll, who combined to save 34 games the previous season, saved 51. In addition, 22-year-old catcher Johnny Bench had a breakout superstar season, blasting 45 home runs, driving in 148 runs, and being voted National League Most Valuable Player, and "Doggie" Perez sparkled with 40 homers and 129 RBIs.

Maybe any manager could have won with those players, but give Sparky Anderson credit; he did it. He immediately quieted the skeptics by winning his first four games. By the first week of May, the Reds had won 22 of 28 games and led the National League West by six games. By July 25 they led by 12½ games. And they finished with a record of 102–60, 14½ games ahead of the Los Angeles Dodgers.

The Reds then swept the Pittsburgh Pirates in the three-game National League Championship Series but lost in the World Series to the Baltimore Orioles (and "Old Man" Frank Robinson), four games to one.

Despite the World Series disappointment, the people of Cincinnati were wild about their Reds and eager for the team's future. They could see even better days ahead. Not only had they accepted "Sparky who?" they came to revere him as a savior, to the point where in just one season he had become the strong man and most powerful force in Cincinnati baseball.

The euphoria in Cincinnati lasted only a short time, as the Reds slipped to a fifth-place finish in 1971, but after the season they pulled off an eight-player trade with the Houston Astros that completed the construction of the Big Red Machine. A key man in the trade for the Astros was slugging first baseman Lee May, but by trading him it enabled the Reds to move Tony Perez from third base to first (and eventually move Rose from the outfield to third base). In the trade, the Reds also acquired second baseman Joe Morgan, who would play himself right into the Hall of Fame.

With their new alignment, the Reds won the National League West by 10½ games over the Dodgers, beat the Pirates three games to two in the NL Championship Series, but again remained unfulfilled as they lost the World Series to the Oakland Athletics, four games to three.

That was the team Will, Ed, and I joined when we flew from Des Moines to Cincinnati. Waiting for us at the airport was the manager of the Holiday Inn in Covington, Kentucky, just a stone's throw to the south of Cincinnati, where we would be put up for the remainder of the season.

We dropped our stuff off at the hotel and went straight to Riverfront Stadium. We found the entrance to the home-team clubhouse, and I was directed to my locker, in which was hanging a fresh, clean white uniform with the number 30 on the back. It was Saturday, August 25, and the St. Louis Cardinals were in for a night game, the second of an important two-game series.

The Reds were in a bit of a tailspin when we joined them. They had lost four straight games, including the series opener to the Cardinals, and fallen four games behind the Dodgers in the National League West, which probably is what led to a minor shakeup that got three young players promoted from Indianapolis.

The whole scene was rather overwhelming for a kid of 23. My head was spinning from the whirlwind few hours since we had left Des Moines and arrived in Cincinnati. I soon learned that Sparky Anderson ruled with an iron fist and that, by his own admission, he played favorites; veterans and superstars got preferential treatment, while rookies and regular players who were not stars—even though they were starters—were practically ignored.

As the new kid on the block, I was intimidated by Sparky and by the parade of stars in the clubhouse, especially the Reds' Big Four:

Johnny Lee Bench was born in Oklahoma City, Oklahoma, on December 7, 1947, six years to the day after the Japanese bombed Pearl Harbor. He was drafted by the Cincinnati Reds right out of Andarko High School in Binger, Oklahoma, in the second round (the 36th pick overall) of the 1965 amateur draft. He reached the major leagues at age 19 and played for 17 seasons, all with the Reds, accumulating 389 home runs and 1,376 runs batted in. He was a key man in helping the Reds win six division titles, four National League pennants, and two World Series. He made 14 All-Star teams and twice was voted National League Most Valuable Player (in 1970, at age 22, he became the youngest player to be voted MVP). He was elected to the Hall of Fame in 1989, his first year of eligibility, receiving 96.42 percent of the votes cast by members of the Baseball Writers' Association of America. ESPN called him "the greatest catcher in baseball history." The Reds permanently retired his No. 5. A bronze statue of Bench in catcher's gear and in the act of throwing out a runner at second base graces the entrance way of the Reds Hall of Fame at Great American Ball Park.

Peter Edward "Pete" Rose, known as "Charlie Hustle" for his hard-nosed, hell-for-leather style of play, is a native Cincinnatian. He signed with his hometown team right out of Western Hills High School before there was a national amateur draft. He is baseball's all-time hits leader with 4,256. He also holds the major league record for singles (3,215), games played (3,562), and at-bats (14,053). He is a former National League Most Valuable Player (1973), a 17-time All-Star, and a three-time batting champion. His was obviously a Hall of Fame–worthy career, but he has been denied admittance to that body for allegedly having bet on baseball and remains permanently ineligible to this day.

Tony Perez (Atanasio Perez Rigal), called "Doggie" or "Big Dog" by his teammates, was born in Ciego de Avila, Cuba. He

Early days with the Cincinnati Reds. (Photo courtesy CEI Sports)

Driving in runs for the Big Red Machine. (Photo courtesy CEI Sports)

The Big Red Machine. That's George Foster, Cesar Geronimo, and me in the back row. In front of us are Dave Concepcion, Sparky Anderson, and Joe Morgan, with Pete Rose and Tony Perez crouching just behind Johnny Bench. (Getty Images)

Here I am with my first wife, Birdie, and our sons, Craig (in my arms) and Ken Jr.
(Photo courtesy CEI Sports)

Tony Perez drove me in to score the winning run in Game 2 of the 1976 World Series.

(AP Images)

Here I am leaping over the fence in Yankee Stadium to pull back a home run. (Getty Images)

Crossing home plate after blasting a two-run homer in Yankee Stadium. (AP Images)

My last stop, the Seattle Mariners, in 1990 and '91. (AP Images)

was discovered in 1960, at age 17, by Cincinnati Reds scout Tony Pacheco and signed for a bonus of the cost of a visa ($2.50) and a plane ticket to Miami, Florida. Doggie's route to the Hall of Fame in 2000 was through Cincinnati, Montreal, Boston, Philadelphia, and Cincinnati again, where he compiled 2,732 hits, 379 home runs, and 1,652 RBIs in a 23-year career. Also in 2000, the Reds permanently retired the Big Dog's No. 24.

Joe Leonard Morgan was the only member of the Big Four who was not an original Red. He was born in Bonham, Texas; raised in Oakland, California; and signed by the Houston Colt .45s (later the Astros). In November 1971 he was part of a blockbuster eight-player trade that proved to be the final bolt in the construction of the Big Red Machine. The diminutive (5'7") Morgan made 10 All-Star teams and won five Gold Gloves. Morgan was elected to the Hall of Fame in 1990. After retiring as an active player, "Little Joe" spent more than two decades as a baseball television analyst for ABC, NBC, and ESPN.

So I was intimidated by those guys and was sitting at my locker that first day trying to process everything that had happened in the past few hours, trying my best to be nonchalant and act as if I belonged, when Sparky approached me and asked me if I was nervous.

"Yes," I replied, "very much."

"You should get a little more nervous," he said, "because you're starting in right field tonight."

Eleven different guys had played right field for the Reds before I got there—even Johnny Bench and my buddy Dan Driessen were briefly pressed into emergency duty at the position—but nobody had taken control of the job. Bobby Tolan started most games in right field, but he was having a bad year, hitting around .200, which was why I got my chance. It was up to me to make the most of it.

Here is the starting lineup Sparky Anderson presented to the umpires in my first major league game:

Pete Rose, lf

Joe Morgan, 2b

Dan Driessen, 3b

Tony Perez, 1b

Johnny Bench, c

Ken Griffey, rf

Cesar Geronimo, cf

Darrel Chaney, ss

Don Gullett, p

The Cardinals lineup included my baseball idol and role model, Lou Brock; Ted Simmons; and Joe Torre. Tim McCarver was to be used as a pinch-hitter. The Cards' starting pitcher was Rick Wise, a hard-throwing veteran right-hander who had come to St. Louis from the Phillies the previous year in a much-publicized and controversial trade for Steve Carlton. Wise had won 15, 13, 17, and 16 games the past four seasons, and with 13 wins already that season, he had five consecutive years with double figures in wins.

I took the field in the top of the first and couldn't help looking around and seeing all the red shirts in the stands. Talk about being nervous. The crowd was huge—50,072 it turned out, more than twice the population of my hometown.

As nervous as I was, I was glad that my first major league at-bat came quickly, in the first inning. Rose started us off with a single, and Morgan followed with another single, sending Rose to third. Morgan then stole second, and Driessen singled both of them home. Perez grounded out, forcing Driessen at second, and Bench also grounded out, sending Perez to second. Then it was my turn, and I hit a ground ball to second baseman Ted Sizemore, who threw me out for the third out. Even though I didn't get a hit, I was glad to put my first major league at-bat behind me.

In the second inning, Driessen batted with the bases loaded and cleared the bases with a double to put us up 5–1. Dan had driven in all five of our runs. I was proud of my pal. Wise was removed for a pinch-hitter in the third, so when I came to bat for the second time in the bottom of the third, the Cardinals had a new pitcher on the mound, a right-hander named Tom Murphy, who served up the pitch that became my first major league hit, a solid line drive double to left.

I got two more at-bats. In the fifth, I beat out an infield single against left-hander Al "the Mad Hungarian" Hrabosky, and in the eighth I hit a tapper in front of the plate off Orlando Pena and was thrown out. All in all, I was pleased with going 2-for-4 in my major league debut and being on the winning side in a 6–4 score.

The two hits in my first game earned me a start in right field again the next day. We beat the Cardinals again, 4–1, and again I was 2-for-4, singles off Reggie Cleveland in the sixth and seventh innings.

After a day off, the Pirates came to town, and they pounded us 8–3, but again I got two hits, a single in the fourth off Bob Moose and another single in the eighth off Bob Johnson. The next day we beat the Pirates 5–3, and I got three hits, a single and double off Nelson Briles and a single off Luke Walker, a left-hander. Since being called up, I had started four consecutive games in right field and had nine hits in 17 at-bats, a .529 average. Obviously, my confidence was sky-high.

I continued to hit: three more knocks against the Padres in San Diego on September 2; the next night, in Houston, a pinch-hit single (with a left-hander pitching against us, Sparky started veteran Andy Kosco in right field) off Ken Forsch in the eighth inning that drove in two runs (my first two major league RBIs) and gave us a 4–3 win; and a triple and two singles on September 4 in a 12–7 beating of the Astros. When I joined the Reds, they were in second place four games behind the Dodgers, but with our win over the Astros, we had taken over first place in the National League West.

I was hitting a torrid .533 (16 hits in 30 at-bats), but I knew my hot streak couldn't last, and it didn't. I went hitless in nine at-bats over the next three games, but I rebounded to get three hits, including my first major league home run (off Roric Harrison), against the Braves in Atlanta in the first game of a doubleheader on September 9.

Two days later, we were home getting ready to welcome the Dodgers in the first of two games. We had a four-game lead over the Dodgers, but they had their two best pitchers, Don Sutton and Claude Osteen, lined up and were hoping to make their move to overtake us.

In the first game of the two, the Dodgers jumped out to an early lead with single runs in the second and third against my old spring-training nemesis, Ross Grimsley. Tony Perez led off the bottom of the fourth with a double and moved to third on a wild pitch. Johnny Bench walked, and I was the next batter. I got into a Sutton fastball and drove it over the fence in right field for a three-run homer and a 3–2 lead.

The Dodgers came back to tie the score in the top of the seventh, but we scored three in the bottom of the eighth and nailed down a 6–3 win.

After the game, one of the reporters asked Sparky Anderson about my home run and the good start to my major league career (I was then batting .429 on 21 hits in 49 at-bats, with two home runs, eight runs batted in, and 12 runs scored).

I was told that Sparky's reply was, "They don't know him that well. They'll get him next year."

I was shocked when I was told of Sparky's response, and perplexed, and more than a little upset. Even my teammate George Foster asked me, "What did you do to Sparky?"

My answer was, and is, nothing that I could think of. I don't remember ever having a cross word with him. In fact, I hardly remember ever having any words, good or bad, with a man who had the reputation of being a nonstop talker. I was baffled when he made those remarks, and I'm still baffled to this day.

The fact is, I feel I played my butt off for Sparky and produced. In that first year, I batted .384, hit three home runs, scored 19 runs, and drove in 14 in 25 games, of which the Reds won 19. Didn't I deserve a little love?

5

HUSTLE

The next thing I knew,
all hell broke loose.

ON MONDAY, SEPTEMBER 24, WE CLINCHED THE 1973 NATIONAL League West championship with a 2–1 victory at home against the San Diego Padres—and without me. Because the Padres started a left-hander, Sparky Anderson, as he had been doing since I arrived, kept me on the bench and started veteran Andy Kosco in right field. That gave me a clue as to what I could expect in the best-of-five National League Championship Series.

I was just happy to be there. I had no guarantee when the Reds brought me up, so I didn't even know I was going to be on the playoff roster. Our opponent in the NLCS would be the New York Mets, who had finished first in the National League East in what was being hailed as a miracle. On July 8 the Mets were in last place, 12½ games out with a record of 34–46. But relief pitcher Tug McGraw told his teammates that "You gotta believe," which became the Mets' rallying cry, and their manager, Yogi Berra, wisely if ungrammatically cautioned one and all that "It ain't over 'til it's over."

The Mets wound up wiping out the entire deficit and jumping over five teams to win their division. It wasn't that they went on some kind of magical winning streak. They won only 48 of their last 81 games and finished with a record of 82–79 and a winning percentage of .509 that is the second lowest of any pennant winner in major league history.

Naturally, we were heavy favorites to win the series and advance to the World Series. Most experts figured we'd win in a walk and that the Mets would be lucky to win a game. The numbers were heavily in our favor. We had scored 741 runs during the season, hit 137 home runs, and stolen 148 bases. The Mets scored 608 runs, hit 85 homers, and stole 27 bases. The Mets had no regulars with a .300

average; we had two, Pete Rose and Tony Perez. The Mets' leading RBI man was Rusty Staub with 76; we had two with more than 100 RBIs, Perez and Johnny Bench. The Mets' home-run leader was John Milner with 23; we had three players with more than that, Bench, Perez, and Joe Morgan.

What the Mets did have was a very good young pitching staff, and two of their top three starters were left-handed, Jerry Koosman and Jon Matlack, which I understood would mean I'd be spending most of the series on the bench.

I did get a start in Game 1, a Saturday in Riverfront Stadium, batting sixth and playing right field because the Mets started a right-hander, Tom Seaver, thank you very much. Veteran Jack Billingham pitched for us, and these two right-handers put on a pitching clinic.

The Mets pushed across a run in the second inning. After the first two batters went out on a fly ball and a strikeout, Billingham walked the eighth batter, Bud Harrelson, and then Seaver himself drove Harrelson home with a line-drive double into the left-center gap.

It appeared that's how the game would end. It was still 1–0 through seven innings. Billingham had allowed just three hits and struck out six, but he remained on the losing end, because Seaver was even better. He had allowed four hits and struck out 11.

Billingham set the Mets down 1-2-3 in the top of the eighth and was scheduled to be the first batter in the bottom of the eighth, but Anderson was left with no choice: he had to send up a pinch-hitter. It was Hal King, who became Seaver's 12th strikeout victim.

We were down to our final five outs as the lineup turned over and Rose batted for the fourth time. He had popped out, flied out, and struck out the first three times, but you know Pete; he always saved his best for last, always was ready to do something dramatic in crunch time, and that time he didn't fail. He had hit only five home runs all season in 752 plate appearances. No matter. We needed a home run, and Pete gave us just that.

The score was tied 1–1.

Seaver came back to make Morgan his 13th strikeout victim and get Dan Driessen on a fly ball, and we went to the ninth.

Tom Hall, a slim left-hander, replaced Billingham. When he walked Staub, Sparky went to the mound to get Hall and bring in Pedro Borbon, who retired the Mets in order.

We came to bat in the bottom of the ninth with the heart of our batting order due up. I was to be the third hitter in the inning, after Perez and Bench. Doggie grounded out to shortstop, and as Bench moved into the batter's box I settled into the on-deck circle. Best seat in the house! I was able to watch up close when J.B. hit a howitzer into the left-field seats.

Game over! Reds win 2–1! Whew!

In Game 2 the next day, I took a seat on the bench and watched as Mets left-hander Jon Matlack tied our bats in knots. He struck out nine and allowed just two hits, both of them by Andy Kosco, who had replaced me in right field.

Except for Staub's solo home run in the fourth, Don Gullett pretty much matched Matlack pitch-for-pitch for five innings, and then Clay Carroll came in to throw three hitless innings. So through eight innings it was almost a carbon copy of Game 1, the Mets ahead 1–0, each team with just two hits. We needed to hold the Mets scoreless in the top of the ninth and break out our ninth-inning lightning in the bottom of the inning as we had done the day before to go up in the series two games to none.

Unfortunately, Tom Hall was brought in to pitch the ninth for us and he had no command that day. After getting the first batter, Wayne Garrett, to hit an easy ground ball to first, he gave up a single to Felix Millan, walked Staub, and was tagged for a single by Cleon Jones that drove home Millan to make it 2–0.

That was all for Hall. Pedro Borbon came in, but he was torched for consecutive singles by Jerry Grote, Don Hahn, and Harrelson.

The Mets had scored four runs, and they put the game away with Matlack firing bullets. He finished up by retiring Morgan, Perez, and Bench in order in the ninth—fly ball, fly ball, strikeout—and the Mets, with their 5–0 victory, had tied the series at one game apiece.

David had slayed Goliath.

Truman had defeated Dewey.

The Washington Generals had beaten the Harlem Globetrotters.

The United States Olympic Hockey Team had upset Russia.

I can only imagine the jubilation in the Mets clubhouse after that victory and Bud Harrelson making an off-the-cuff remark, intending it as a joke, that would come back to bite him when a reporter carried the comment to our dressing room.

Apparently, Harrelson had this kind of self-deprecating humor, so when someone asked him about Matlack's dominance over our powerful hitters, Harrelson supposedly said, "They looked like me hitting."

Funny line! Not meant to be insulting? Harmless?

Not if you were just beaten. Not if you were humiliated on the field, got only two singles and were tied at one game apiece with a team you figured to roll over. And certainly not if you were Pete Rose!

By that time Rose's reputation as Charley Hustle had taken hold, the perception that he was a hard loser, a battler, a guy who didn't accept defeat graciously, who would fight you at every turn for every run, every victory. Only three years earlier, remember, he had bowled over catcher Ray Fosse in a play at the plate during the All-Star Game, and Fosse was never the same player again. Rose had that reputation to uphold, and he upheld it at every turn.

Ever since he knocked over Fosse, Pete would be booed in every opponent's ballpark, and he loved it. It motivated him; as if he needed any more motivation. The more they booed, the harder he played.

I was Pete's teammate for six seasons, and he was the most competitive, most driven, most determined player I have ever been around. And the most insecure!

So when Harrelson's comment got back to him, everyone figured Pete was going to use it as fuel to motivate his teammates if he got the opportunity. But I never heard Pete say anything negative about Harrelson or promise to "get" him. The only thing that mattered to Pete, the only thing that always mattered to Pete, was winning the game.

I don't understand why people think that because he played so hard and looked cocky that Pete was out to hurt people or that he made threats against opponents. Pete never talked that way. He never held a grudge against anyone; he just played hard all the time. That was just his style.

Game 2 had been on a Sunday. There was no off-day as the scene shifted to New York's Shea Stadium for Game 3 on a beautiful Indian summer, sun-splashed Monday afternoon. Those of us in the Reds clubhouse and dugout figured Rose was still seething over losing Game 2 and over Harrelson's remark, and he was waiting for his chance to strike.

To make matters worse, things were not going our way on the field in Game 3. Ross Grimsley started for us against another left-hander, Jerry Koosman, for the Mets, meaning that I was spending another game on the bench. Sparky again played Andy Kosco in my place in right field. His reason? "Morgan can't hit Koosman, so you're not playing."

How's that for logic? I suppose he was trying to say that he wanted to limit the number of left-handed hitters in our lineup against left-handed pitchers, but why single me out? I proved during the season that I could hit left-handers.

Rusty Staub hit a home run in the first inning to give the Mets a 1–0 lead. In the second, they exploded. A walk and two singles loaded the bases with one out. Wayne Garrett drove in a run with a sacrifice fly. Felix Millan drove in two more with a single. With Staub due up, Sparky removed Grimsley and replaced him with Tom Hall, but Staub wrecked the strategy by belting his second home run in two innings, a three-run shot that gave the Mets a 6–0 lead.

By the fifth inning, we were down 9–2 when Rose came to bat with one out and nobody on base. It appeared that his anger, frustration, and disappointment were about to spill over when he hit a line-drive single to center. And when Morgan followed with a ground ball to first baseman John Milner, Pete's chance had come.

Milner fielded the ball smoothly and fired a strike to shortstop Harrelson covering second base, the throw beating Rose by plenty. But Pete wasn't going to take that lying down…or standing up. As Harrelson came in contact with second base and relayed the ball back to Milner to complete the double play, Rose went barreling into Harrelson, knocking him to the ground.

The next thing I knew, all hell broke loose. Rose and Harrelson were rolling around in the dirt around second base, both benches and bullpens had emptied, and players were streaming onto the field, ready to do battle. Scuffles between Reds and Mets players were springing up all around Shea Stadium, typical baseball melees, which means mostly standing around and talking.

I'm not a fighter, but I was on the field with everybody else. It's what you do. You have to support your teammate, whether you think he's right or wrong. But that doesn't mean you have to act crazy and start throwing punches at opponents, and I didn't. Unfortunately others did.

I witnessed one brawl between relief pitchers, our guy Pedro Borbon and the Mets' Buzz Capra. Borbon hauled off and slugged Capra when he wasn't looking. Even Sparky said later that Pedro was out of line. In any case, in the course of the scuffle Borbon and Capra both had their caps fly off their heads and land on the ground.

After an uncertain peace had been restored, Cesar Geronimo and I were walking off the field alongside Borbon, who reached down and picked up a cap and put it on his head. He didn't realize he had picked up Capra's hat by mistake.

I said, "Pedro, you got the wrong hat," and Geronimo said the same thing to him in Spanish. Borbon took it off his head, looked at the cap, and put it back on his head, and we said it to him again: "No, you have the wrong hat on."

That's when Pedro took the hat off his head, looked at it again, and realized it was a Mets cap. He was so mad he took a bite out of it and tore the cap into pieces. The next thing I saw was Cleon Jones walking behind Pedro picking up pieces of Capra's hat.

When the ruckus had ended and we took the field, fans started raining all kinds of garbage down on the field—fruit, bottles, cans, anything they could get their hands on that they could hurl. A whiskey bottle just missed Pete Rose standing in left field. When he saw that, Sparky pulled his team off the field for their protection and said he wouldn't have them take the field again until the crowd had been warned and he felt it was safe to return.

Chub Feeney, the president of the National League, was at the game, sitting near the Mets dugout. He ordered the Mets to make an announcement on the loudspeaker that if the fans didn't stop throwing objects on the field, the Mets would forfeit the game. When that didn't do the trick, Feeney asked Mets manager Yogi Berra to go out to left field and appeal to the fans.

Yogi, Willie Mays (who had been traded to the Mets a year earlier to finish out his career in New York), Cleon Jones, Tom Seaver, and Rusty Staub did as the league president requested, and the fans stopped throwing things. That's when Anderson sent his team back on the field and the game continued.

Whatever Rose had hoped to achieve by upending Harrelson didn't work, as neither team scored after the incident. The Mets completed the 9–2 victory and went ahead in the series two games to one.

We were up against it, one defeat from elimination with the last two games of the series to be played in New York. Game 4 was another matchup of veteran left-handers, Fred Norman for us and George Stone for them, so once more I was going to be watching the game from our dugout.

Both Norman and Stone were outstanding. The Mets scored first with a run in the third on two walks and an RBI single by Felix Millan. And that was all they got off Norman, who left after five innings having allowed just that one run and one hit. Don Gullett replaced him and pitched four shutout innings, allowing only two hits.

Meanwhile, we tied the score in the seventh on Perez's home run off Stone, who was lifted with two outs in the inning and the score tied 1–1.

That's how it stood through the ninth inning, the 10th, and the 11th as Tug McGraw pitched four and one-third scoreless innings, matching zeros first with Gullett and then with Clay Carroll.

In the 12th right-hander Harry Parker replaced McGraw and I got my chance, leading off the inning as a pinch-hitter for Carroll. I hit a drive to left field that was caught and that brought up Rose. And wouldn't you know Pete would come through again, even if it was a day later than he had planned. He belted his second home run of the series (he batted .381 for the series) to put us up 2–1. When Borbon came in and, wearing his own hat, retired the Mets in order in the bottom of the 12th, we had tied the series at two games each, and it all came down to Game 5 the following day.

With a pitching rematch of Game 1, Jack Billingham against Tom Seaver, Game 5 figured to be a classic. It wasn't. Billingham couldn't have picked a worse day to be off his game as he gave up two runs in the first. The Mets knocked him out with four more runs in the fifth to take a 6–2 lead. While he wasn't at his best,

Seaver was plenty good enough, leaving with one out in the ninth leading, 7–2.

Tug McGraw got the final two outs before they went crazy at Shea Stadium while we walked away terribly disappointed but still believing we were the better team.

I'll take my share of the blame. I managed one hit in four at-bats, a double in the fourth, my only hit in the series in seven at-bats.

I did, however, manage one distinction, and it's one for trivia buffs.

Q: Who made the putout on Willie Mays' final at-bat in the National League?

A: I did.

Let me make it clear that Mays went on to play in the 1973 World Series with the Mets against the Oakland Athletics, and he was 2-for-7, the final at-bat of his fabulous career coming in Game 3 in Shea Stadium. With two outs and a runner on second in the 10th inning of a 2–2 tie, Willie batted for Tug McGraw. Paul Lindblad pitched, and Mays hit a ground ball to shortstop Bert Campaneris, who flipped to second baseman Ted Kubiak for a force-out.

My trivia question stipulates his last at-bat in the *National League*.

Well, it came in the bottom of the eighth inning of Game 5 of the 1973 National League Championship Series also at Shea Stadium. Ross Grimsley pitched, and Mays lifted a fly ball to right field and I caught it. I wish now I had stuffed that ball in my pocket and kept it all these years.

SETBACK

Many have called the 1975 World Series the greatest ever and Game 6 the greatest game ever played.

EXCEPT FOR THE DISAPPOINTMENT OF LOSING TO THE NEW York Mets in the National League Championship Series, I was pleased with my first major league experience. In 25 games, I had batted an impressive .384 (33 hits in 86 at-bats)—with five doubles, one triple, and three home runs—scored 19 runs, drove in 14, and stole four bases. I felt confident that I had shown enough to warrant more playing time in 1974 and looked forward to the start of the new season.

In spring training I was taken aback when Sparky Anderson told me he wanted me to bunt more that season in order for the Reds to take advantage of my speed. To help me improve my bunting he asked the incomparable Rod Carew, then with the Minnesota Twins and one of the game's most accomplished bunters ever, to work with me. Rod graciously agreed and generously gave me his time for a few lessons. That whole spring, all I did was bunt.

We opened the 1974 season on April 4 at home against the Atlanta Braves. It was an exciting time, not only because it was the start of a new baseball season, but because Hank Aaron was about to break Babe Ruth's all-time career home-run record of 714. He had finished the 1973 season with 713 home runs, and it was Cincinnati's good fortune that the schedule had the Braves in town for three games to open the season on April 4, 6, and 7.

The Braves had announced that Aaron would be held out of the series against us so that he could have the opportunity to tie and/or break the record in the Braves' home opener on April 8. That's when commissioner Bowie Kuhn stepped in and, for the good and the integrity of the game, ordered Aaron to play in at least two games in Cincinnati (the number of games was based on Aaron's pattern of play in 1973, when he had appeared in two-thirds of the Braves' games).

Batting fourth in the Braves lineup, Aaron came to the plate against Jack Billingham in the first inning, with runners on first and second and one out. The count went to 3–1, and Hank hit the next pitch over the head of left fielder Pete Rose and into the seats for career home run number 714, putting him in a tie with Babe Ruth. After that historic home run, it didn't seem that Hank was trying too hard, as he grounded to third base in the third inning, walked in the fifth (Billingham didn't seem too interested either in getting his name in the record books as the pitcher who gave up home run number 715), and flied out in the seventh before being removed from the game.

Hank sat out the second game of the series and, as ordered, started the third game. He batted three times, struck out looking twice, and grounded out to third base before being removed. That left him in the perfect position to break the record the following night in the Braves' home opener in Atlanta, which is exactly what he did with home run 715 off Al Downing of the Los Angeles Dodgers.

I had been in the Opening Day starting lineup batting sixth and playing right field. I was hitless in four at-bats and struck out three times, but despite my failure and Aaron's historic three-run first-inning bomb—which I had the opportunity to observe from my position in right field—we won the game 7–6 in 11 innings. Isn't that what's most important? Besides, this was only one game; still 161 to go.

We had the next day off and played our second game on April 6. Again, I was in right field batting sixth. The Braves had jumped out to an early lead and were ahead of us 5–3 when I came to bat in the fifth inning with two runners on base. I promptly drove both of them in with a triple to tie the score at 5–5. I didn't get another hit, but we scored twice in the seventh and won the game 7–5. It was a very good day.

After that I went hitless in my next eight at-bats, and I started to think about what Sparky Anderson had said the year before, after I hit a home run off Don Sutton to beat the Dodgers: *They don't know him that well. They'll get him next year.*

Was Sparky's prediction coming true, or was I simply another innocent victim of baseball's sophomore jinx?

By May 11 I had played in 19 games and was batting only .158 (9-for-57 with no doubles, one triple, no home runs, five runs batted in, and two stolen bases) when I got the bad news from Sparky Anderson: he was sending me back to Indianapolis. He said it was because I needed to work on my bunting.

It's never easy to be sent back to the minor leagues after you have experienced the luxury of major league life—the first-class hotels, the major league meal money, the convenience of air travel as opposed to buses. When you're sent back to the minors and you lose all that, you're faced with two choices: you can work your butt off and force them to take you back up as soon as possible, or you can feel sorry for yourself and sit around brooding and pouting. If you choose the latter, you better start thinking about finding another profession, because you're going to be cooked in this one. Fortunately, I chose the former.

In 43 games with the Indians, I batted .333 (54-for-162) with six doubles, four triples, five home runs, 18 RBIs, and 12 stolen bases, which earned me a return ticket to Cincinnati.

When I returned on July 2, I found the Reds seven and a half games behind the National League West–leading Los Angeles Dodgers. Led by manager Walter Alston, the team boasted a solid infield of first baseman Steve Garvey, second baseman Davey Lopes, shortstop Bill Russell, and third baseman Ron "the Penguin" Cey, and a pitching staff that included starters Don Sutton, Tommy John, and Andy Messersmith, with the iron man, Mike Marshall, in the bullpen.

After I returned to Cincinnati, I didn't quite do enough to have people compare me to my homeboy Stan Musial, but my hitting did improve, and I feel I did my part in helping the Reds begin to turn around their season. Five days after I arrived, we went on a streak and won eight out of nine games. By August 18 we had won 29 out of 47 and cut the Dodgers' lead to two and a half games.

We kept the pressure on and avoided elimination by winning six straight games from September 24 to 29. We were finally mathematically eliminated on October 1, the next-to-last day of the season, and finished four games behind the Dodgers, who won 102 games. But we ended up winning 98 games, the second-most wins in Major League Baseball. Unfortunately baseball had not yet instituted the wild-card format, and we were left out of the postseason. Still, the season wasn't a total loss.

Personally, my confidence had returned with my strong second half. After I came back from Indianapolis, I hit .282 in 69 games and finished with a respectable .251 batting average.

As a team, we also took solace from a strong second half, and we believed that would hold us in good stead the following season.

We started 1975 on a win-one-lose-one treadmill. On Friday, May 2, after 24 games, we were 12–12 and sitting in third place, four games out of first. It was just about that time that Sparky dropped Joe Morgan from the No. 2 hole in the batting order to No. 3 and moved me up to No. 2, which is how our lineup remained for most of the rest of the season.

I was a rookie hitting between Pete Rose and Joe Morgan. My strike zone was as big as the Monongahela River. Their strike zones were as big as a postage stamp. I was always being teased about all the infield hits I got. Well, the reason was, I seemed to always be hitting with two strikes on me. I wasn't afraid to hit with two strikes, but it seemed that when I had two strikes on me and the next pitch would be six inches off the plate or up in my eyes or down by my shins, I knew that if I took it the umpire would shout "Strike three!" So I had to try to make contact in order to survive and keep the at-bat alive. When I did, I'd beat the ball into the ground, and because I could outrun anybody, I'd beat the ball out, and that's how I got so many infield hits. Tony Perez started calling me "KIP," which meant "Keep It in Play." That's how I survived, and that's how I got the reputation for accumulating so many infield hits. They started counting my infield hits, and I think I had about 36 or 38 in 1975 and 1976.

Soon after Sparky moved me into the No. 2 hole in 1975, we went on a tear and won 21 of 31 games and moved into first place on June 3. Then we really took off. On September 7 we led the Dodgers in the National League West by 20½ games. We ended the season with a record of 108–54 and a 20-game lead in the division after winning 96 of our last 138 games.

It was my first full season with the Reds, and I felt I established myself as a bona fide major leaguer. I batted .305, hit 15 doubles, nine triples (tied for sixth in the league), and four home runs. I also drove in 46 runs and stole 16 bases.

For the third time in six years we hooked up with the Pittsburgh Pirates in the National League Championship Series. The Pirates always played us tough, and with guys like Willie Stargell, Dave Parker, Al Oliver, and Manny Sanguillen, they weren't going to be a pushover. But the Big Red Machine had hit its stride, and there was no stopping us.

We rolled over the Pirates in three straight by scores of 8–3, 6–1, and 5–3. I had four hits in the series (at least one in each game) in 12 at-bats.

In Game 1 I doubled in two runs in the third inning to break a 2–2 tie and drove in another run with a ground-out in the fifth.

In Game 2 I singled in a run and stole three bases (we stole seven as a team).

In Game 3 I singled in four at-bats.

We were moving on to the World Series against the Boston Red Sox. It was my first, and I couldn't help but wonder how I would fare on the big stage. I was looking forward to the experience, excited but apprehensive.

Many have called the 1975 World Series the greatest ever and Game 6 the greatest game ever played. I'll leave that to the expert veteran observers. What I can tell you is that playing in that World Series was everything I thought it would be…and more.

If we were the Big Red Machine, the Red Sox were hardly the Little Engine That Could.

They had a powerful offense that included three future Hall of Famers (Carl Yastrzemski, Carlton Fisk, and Jim Rice); two gifted young players (Rice and Fred Lynn) who each batted higher than .300, hit more than 20 home runs, and drove in more than 100 runs; plus Cecil Cooper, a .311 hitter, and Dwight Evans and Rico Petrocelli. They also had three pitchers (Luis Tiant, Rick Wise, and Bill Lee) who combined for 54 wins.

The Red Sox appeared to be a without a weakness.

The World Series began in Boston, in the antiquated but iconic Fenway Park, with its fabled left-field wall, the Green Monster. Fenway is supposed to be a hitter's paradise, but not that day, as Don Gullett for us and Luis Tiant for them baffled and completely dominated hitters for six scoreless innings, Gullett with his blazing fastball, Tiant with a variety of deliveries from a series of different angles and release points and an array of contortions, stops and starts, and gyrations.

The Cuban-born, cigar-chomping Tiant was a foreboding and sinister figure with a large belly, a barrel chest, and a drooping Fu Manchu mustache who peered at hitters with piercing, penetrating eyes. He was a man of many deliveries. He might throw overhand on one pitch, sidearm on the next pitch, and underhand on the next pitch. He might spin it, he might sink it, he might float it, and always he would surprise you. Hitting against him was like eating soup with a fork.

Before releasing the ball El Tiante would pivot on his right leg, spin completely around until he faced second base, and then wheel and throw, giving the hitter the impression that he was never sure exactly where his pitches were going. But he *was* sure…always.

Somehow we managed to get five hits off Tiant—two by Joe Morgan, two by George Foster, and my double with two outs in the top of the seventh (unfortunately it came after Foster had singled and been thrown out attempting to steal second).

In the bottom of the seventh, the Red Sox exploded. A walk and five singles knocked out Gullett as they scored six runs. And that's how it ended: Boston 6, Cincinnati 0.

Things were much different in Game 2. On a terrible New England night in which the game was halted by rain for 27 minutes, we got a chance to show our resolve and our resourcefulness. Left-hander Bill Lee had picked up where Luis Tiant left off, holding us scoreless through three innings and to just one run and four hits through eight while the Red Sox scored a run in the first and another in the sixth, leaving them three outs away from taking a commanding 2–0 lead in the Series.

When Bench led off the top of the ninth with a double to right field, Lee was lifted and replaced by Dick Drago, a hard-throwing right-hander who promptly got Tony Perez to ground out to short, moving Bench to third with the tying run, and George Foster to fly out to left field, too shallow for Bench to tag up and score. It was up to Dave Concepcion to keep our hopes alive. Drago threw him two fastballs that Davey couldn't catch up to. He swung and missed the first one for a strike, took the second one for a ball. Drago threw another fastball, and Davey chopped it toward second base. The Red Sox second baseman Denny Doyle raced to his right, backhanded the ball cleanly, and fired to first. But his throw was too late. Davey was burning, the outcome of the game, maybe even the whole World Series, depending on his speed. He beat the throw, and Bench scored the tying run.

Then it was my turn at bat. On the first pitch, Concepcion, using his speed again, took off for second base and slid in safely with a steal. With first base open, I wondered if the Red Sox would avoid the righty pitcher vs. lefty hitter and either bring in a left-hander or walk me intentionally. They did neither, possibly because the hitter on deck, Cesar Geronimo, was also left-handed.

I was glad to have the chance to drive in the go-ahead run, and I drove a fastball against the Green Monster as Concepcion scored easily. It was the first time in the Series a Reds batter had reached the inviting and easily reachable wall, and it proved to be the winning run when Rawly Eastwick retired the Red Sox in order in the bottom of the ninth.

We had pulled even in the Series one game apiece, and we flew home to Cincinnati by charter feeling pretty good about our situation. I was in good spirits until I picked up the Cincinnati *Enquirer* the next morning and read the headline: BENCH DOUBLE BRINGS WINNER.

Bench double? Are you kidding me? I was baffled and mystified.

Bench's double had started the ninth-inning rally. I gave him all the credit in the world for that. But he didn't drive in a run. He didn't even score the winning run. He scored the tying run. Dave Concepcion scored the winning run, and the guy who drove him in was me.

I learned later that the *Enquirer* was bombarded with telephone calls complaining about the headline, and the conspiracy theorists were saying that the headline was driven by racism, that the paper was giving Bench credit for winning the game because he was white and refusing to give me the credit because I was black. Those charges didn't come from me. I never have thought that way, not then and not now. But I was angry that I wasn't getting the credit I was due.

Largely because of the Green Monster, Fenway Park has the reputation of being a launching pad, and there was so much speculation about how that would all play out in the World Series. Would each game be a shootout? Would home-run records fall?

Funny game, baseball! Not one home run was hit by either side in the first two games of the '75 Series, both played at Fenway Park.

In Game 3 at Cincinnati's Riverfront Stadium, six home runs were hit, three by each side.

Bench hit a two-run shot in the fourth, and Concepcion and Geronimo went back-to-back off Rick Wise in the fifth, giving us a 4–1 lead. Carlton Fisk had hit a home run for the Red Sox in the second. Bernie Carbo hit one in the seventh to cut our lead to 5–3. And with one out in the top of the ninth, Dwight Evans belted a two-run bomb off Rawly Eastwick to tie the score at 5–5.

That's where it stood in the bottom of the 10th when Cesar Geronimo led off the inning with a sharp single up the middle. That's when Sparky decided to play manager. He sent Ed Armbrister up to hit for Eastwick with the express purpose of sacrificing the winning run to second base. What happened next may have been the play that decided the World Series.

Armbrister bunted, the ball kangaroo-hopping high in the air, either because of the artificial turf or because it hit home plate. As Red Sox catcher Carlton Fisk jumped out from behind the plate to field the bunt, Armbrister started toward first, took one step, and stopped, fearing he might be charged with interference. There was brief incidental contact between Armbrister and Fisk, who shoved Armbrister aside and fired to second base in an attempt to force Geronimo. But the throw sailed high and flew into center field as Geronimo raced to third and Armbrister to second and both managers raced to offer the umpires advice on how the play should be ruled.

Red Sox manager Darrell Johnson argued that Armbrister obstructed/impeded Fisk and he should be ruled out and Geronimo sent back to first base. Sparky Anderson argued that the rule states it is obstruction only if the runner fails to avoid a fielder attempting to field a batted ball, and Armbrister clearly was attempting to avoid impeding Fisk so the play should stand, runners on second and third, nobody out.

Home-plate umpire Larry Barnett agreed with (was snowed by?) Sparky, and we had runners on second and third with no outs. With Pete Rose due up, the Red Sox replaced right-hander Jim Willoughby with Roger Moret, a tall, pencil-thin left-hander who came in with instructions to walk Rose, intentionally loading the bases and setting up a force at home. That left it up to me to get the winning run home from third. Or did it? Much to my surprise, and chagrin, Sparky called me back and sent Merv Rettenmund, a veteran right-handed batter, up as a pinch-hitter.

I couldn't believe it. Rettenmund, playing sparingly all season, had batted .239. I was a .305 hitter, had proven I could hit left-handers as well as right-handers, and Sparky hadn't pinch-hit for me since July. I didn't understand that at all, because he didn't pinch-hit for me against Matlack, Koosman, or Tommy John, who I hit better than anybody. He didn't pinch-hit for me against Doug Rau, Joe Sambito, or Gary Lavelle, all good left-handers. Roger Moret? Come on! I was crushed, dissed by Sparky one more time.

Rettenmund struck out, but Joe Morgan followed with a line-drive single to center to score Geronimo with the winning run. In the victorious clubhouse, I was angry and hurt, but I smiled through my pain. After all, we won the game.

Game 4 was another nail-biter. The Red Sox started Luis Tiant on three days' rest. Our pitcher was left-hander Fred Norman.

Facing Tiant in Game 1 and hitting against his repertory of gyrations, contortions, stops and starts, and changes of speed obviously helped, because we reached him for two runs in the first inning. Pete started us off with a single, and I drove a ball to the left-center gap to score him. But I tried to stretch a double into a triple and was thrown out at third, a baseball no-no (you never want to make the first out of an inning or the third out of an inning at third base). I also probably cost us a big inning, as Morgan followed with a walk and Bench doubled him home.

The Red Sox began pounding on Norman in the fourth inning, knocked him out, and continued pounding on his reliever, Pedro Borbon. When the inning was over, they had scored five runs and taken a 5–2 lead. We battled right back in the bottom of the inning to score two runs on a single by George Foster, a double by Dave Concepcion, and a triple by Cesar Geronimo. There still were five innings left, so this looked like it was turning into a shootout of two great offenses. Wrong!

Clay Carroll and Rawly Eastwick combined to give us a chance to win by holding the Red Sox to no runs and two hits over the last five innings. And Tiant seemed to get his second wind and regain his magic touch in the fifth, holding us to no runs and three hits over the last five innings. The Red Sox held on to their 5–4 lead and tied the Series at two games apiece, Tiant the winning pitcher in both his team's victories. It was the third straight game decided by one run.

As it often is in a seven-game series, Game 5 was pivotal. Whichever team won would hold a lead of three games to two and would need to win just one of the last two games to win baseball's championship. The game was more critical for us than the Red Sox. If the Red Sox lost, they at least would have the home-field advantage in the last two games. If we lost we would have to sweep the last two games in enemy territory.

After three straight nail-biters, we needed something close to a "laugher," and we got it in Game 5, thanks mostly to the outstanding pitching of Don Gullett, who gave us eight and two-thirds superb innings. He struck out seven and allowed just two runs and five hits. One of the runs and three of the hits came in the ninth inning, and Rawly Eastwick had to come in and get the last out.

We had helped ease Gullett's burden by scoring single runs in the fourth, fifth, and eighth innings and three runs in the sixth. The final score, 6–2, was a welcome respite after the previous three games. We were up three games to two going to Boston for Game 6 and, if necessary, Game 7.

Friday, October 17, was scheduled as a day off. We were supposed to have a brief workout at Fenway Park, but it rained and the workout was canceled.

It rained again on Saturday, October 18. Game called.

It poured rain on Sunday, October 19. Game called.

It rained buckets on Monday, October 20. Game called. The rain was reaching biblical proportions.

Finally, the rain stopped on Tuesday, October 21, the sun peaked through the clouds, and it was game on.

You might say that all that waiting only intensified the magnitude of Game 6 and brought about the anxiety that made it "the greatest game ever played."

The rain was a break for the Red Sox. Instead of having to wait for Game 7 to bring Luis Tiant back, and then on only three days' rest for the second straight start, it enabled them to bring him back in Game 6 on five days' rest. Our starter was young Gary Nolan, a 15-game winner during the season who had pitched four innings in Game 3, allowing a run and three hits.

The Red Sox jumped on Nolan almost immediately. Gary retired the first two batters in the bottom of the first, but then Yastrzemski and Fisk singled and Fred Lynn blasted a tremendous three-run home run just to my right and over my head. Just like that, we were down 3–0 and forced to play catch-up. The only good thing was that it was still early; there was plenty of baseball to be played and plenty of time to make up the deficit.

We managed to solve Tiant and catch up in the fifth. With one out, Armbrister drew a walk and Rose followed with a single. I drove both runners in with a triple (this time I made sure I reached third safely), and after Morgan popped to third for the second out, Bench came through with a clutch single that got me home and we were tied 3–3, setting the stage for some amazing, high-drama, stomach-churning baseball.

I led off the seventh with a ground-ball single to right. Morgan followed with a single. Runners on first and second with no outs! No sacrificing here, not with Bench, Perez, and Foster ready to take dead aim at the Green Monster. Both Bench and Perez flirted with that wall, so inviting and so close you felt you could reach out and touch it from the batter's box, but so close I couldn't tag up and advance on Bench's drive. I did move up to third on Perez's drive, but I reached there with two outs, and we needed a hit to get me home. Luckily Foster got that hit, a double to right field, the deep part of the ballpark, scoring Morgan and me.

Geronimo led off the eighth with a home run that knocked Tiant out of the game and boosted our lead to 6–3. We needed only six more outs to wrap up the game and begin the celebration. But the Red Sox had other ideas.

Lynn led off the bottom of the eighth with a single. Rico Petrocelli drew a walk, which was Sparky's signal to go to his bullpen one more time. Eastwick replaced Borbon. He struck out Evans and got Rick Burleson on a line drive to left. Two down. One more out would get us out of that jam. The Red Sox sent up a pinch-hitter for pitcher Roger Moret, none other than my old buddy Bernie Carbo. Bernie and I went back to spring training 1972, when he was with the Reds and I was on the big league roster.

Carbo was a popular and colorful figure. He also was a controversial one. Bernie could always hit. Sparky Anderson managed Bernie in the minor leagues at Asheville and often said he was one of his favorite players. Carbo was blessed with a world of talent. He also was cursed with a troubled lifestyle. He had been selected two months before his 18th birthday by the Reds in the first round of the 1965 amateur draft, the 16th pick overall. Five years later, he batted .310 with 21 home runs and 63 RBIs in 125 games and finished second in the voting for National League Rookie of the Year. The following year his average plummeted 91 points to .219, his home runs dropped from 21 to five, and his RBIs sank from 63 to 20. It was clear his lifestyle had caught up with him. A year later, he was on his way out of town.

Carbo, still only 27, was with his third team trying to hang on and prolong his career (he ended up playing his last five seasons with five different teams). With the Red Sox, he was used mostly as a platoon outfielder and pinch-hitter and put up his best numbers since his rookie year, a .257 average, 15 home runs, and 50 RBIs. He had already made his mark in the Series with a pinch-hit home run in Game 3, and suddenly he was in a big spot, the tying run at the plate with time running out on the Red Sox.

The count went to 2–2, and on the next pitch Bernie took one of the worst swings I have ever seen a big-leaguer take, but he somehow managed to get his bat on the ball—how, I'll never know—hitting it practically out of Bench's mitt and just tipping it to stay in the at-bat. And then on the next pitch, *bam!* He hit a bomb, a three-run homer into the center-field seats, no cheapie, to tie the game at 6–6, and the noise at Fenway Park was so loud I couldn't hear myself think.

From that point on the pressure was stifling, mostly for the Red Sox, because for them it was win or go home. In the top of the ninth, we went out in order. In the bottom, the Red Sox loaded the bases with nobody out and failed to score.

In the 10th, we got a man on second but couldn't bring him around. The Red Sox went in order in the bottom half.

The fans were going crazy. So was Pete Rose, who was enjoying every minute of the game and telling that to everybody who came near him.

Pete loved to talk. He talked all the time. He'd talk to anybody—teammates, opponents, coaches, fans. I could see him from right field talking to any runner who reached third base, talking to the Red Sox third-base coach Don Zimmer, who, like Pete, was from Cincinnati. I could see Pete talking to everybody; I just couldn't hear what he was saying. Later I found out that he kept telling everybody how great the game was.

"Isn't this great?" he said to Don Zimmer.

"Have you ever been in such a great game?" he asked Carlton Fisk.

"This is the greatest game I've ever played in," he told Carl Yastrzemski.

In the top of the 11th, Rose was hit by a pitch. My job was to bunt him along to second base. I bunted but didn't get it far enough away from Fisk, who threw to second to force Pete. Morgan then hit into a double play.

The Red Sox went one, two, three in the bottom of the 11th.

To start the 12th inning, the Red Sox brought in one of their top pitchers, 19-game winner Rick Wise, who had been Boston's starter in Game 3. He retired the ever-dangerous Bench on a foul pop to the catcher, but Perez and Foster hit back-to-back singles. Concepcion flied to right field, and Geronimo struck out swinging and we played on, into the bottom of the 12th.

The clock said 12:34 AM as Carlton Fisk stepped into the batter's box to face Pat Darcy, who had entered the game in the 10th inning and had retired all six batters the Red Sox put up against him. His first pitch was a ball. The game was four hours old.

On Darcy's next pitch Fisk swung and sent a drive headed toward the Green Monster in left field. I knew it had the distance to leave the park. It was just a question of fair or foul. From my vantage point in right field it looked like it was fair, but I didn't have a good angle, and I was hoping I was wrong. We were all hoping it would be foul. Fisk hit a screamer, a rocket heading toward the Monster. It's only 310 feet down the line, and because the ball was hit so hard, it didn't have a chance to hook foul. We were hoping it would miss the foul pole, but it didn't, and the next thing I knew the ball bounced off the pole and came straight down right into George Foster's glove, and the Red Sox had tied the Series.

There would be a sudden-death seventh game the next night. We were disappointed, of course, but we weren't beat. Far from it! We knew we were going to win the next day. That was always our mind-set. If we lost a big game, we just figured we'd get 'em tomorrow. That's the way we looked at it. It was a day-to-day thing with us. We never worried about the situation. We played them tough, they played us tough. We had some big hits, they had some big hits. But we figured we'd win out in the end.

So it was Don Gullett vs. Bill Lee in Game 7, one of those "there's no tomorrow" type of games with all hands on deck out of the bullpen.

Gullett got through the first two innings with no problem, but in the third he had all kinds of problems, especially his control, which was not at all like him. It was baffling, because between four walks, one intentional, and two singles, he got three outs on strikeouts. Still the Red Sox had jumped out to a 3–0 lead, and once again we were forced to play catch-up.

We weren't having much success against Lee early. Through the first five innings he held us scoreless. We finally broke through in the sixth on Perez's two-run homer and knocked Lee out in the seventh when we tied the score. I singled with one out, stole second, and scored on Rose's single. So it was 3–3 going into the bottom of the seventh.

Once Gullett left for a pinch-hitter, our bullpen did a masterful job of holding the Red Sox hitters scoreless in their bandbox of a ballpark. Gullett rebounded from his third-inning problems to pitch a scoreless fourth before turning it over to the bullpen. Jack Billingham worked a scoreless fifth and sixth, allowing just one hit. Clay Carroll worked a hitless and scoreless seventh and eighth.

In the top of the ninth I led off with my second consecutive walk, moved to second on a sacrifice, to third on an infield out, and scored on Morgan's single to center. I had scored the tying run and the go-ahead run.

All that was needed was for us to get three outs to celebrate the Reds' first world championship in 35 years, and Will McEnaney came in to nail it down with a one-two-three ninth for his second save of the Series.

It felt good to be a member of a world championship team. So good, we all figured why not do it again the next year?

7
REPEAT

We were, after all,
the Big Red Machine.

WITH JUST A FEW MINOR CHANGES, THE CINCINNATI REDS team that reported to Tampa for spring training in 1976 was essentially the same that had won "the greatest World Series ever played" against the Boston Red Sox. As a matter of fact, I had seen very few changes in personnel since I first joined the Reds in 1973.

Of the eight regular position players, five were homegrown by the Reds (Joe Morgan and Cesar Geronimo from Houston and George Foster from San Francisco came in trades), and despite their ages, the eight were major league veterans with résumés as winners. I was the last of the eight to arrive and, at 26, the youngest. Except for Pete Rose (35), Tony Perez (34), and Morgan (32), every other starter was younger than 30. Rose came to the Reds in 1963, Perez a year later, Bench in 1967, Concepcion in 1970, Foster in 1971, and Morgan and Geronimo in 1972. I came along a year after that.

All eight of us had played an important role in winning the 1975 World Series, and all eight were determined and confident that we would win it again.

We were, after all, the Big Red Machine.

We opened the season winning our first four games, fell back to a record of 12–10, jockeyed for first place in the National League West with the Dodgers and Astros through April and May, and took over the top spot for good on May 31.

In my first few years with the Reds, I had usually batted sixth or seventh in the order. And then in 1975, Sparky started using me in the No. 2 hole and dropped Joe Morgan from second to third. By 1976 that was pretty much the norm—Rose leading off, me second, Morgan third, Perez fourth, Bench fifth, etc. I liked hitting second, and it seemed to agree with me, but when Sparky made the move, he did it with one caveat. Morgan had told him he couldn't hit if I was running, so if I got on base and Morgan was at bat, I was told not to attempt to steal second base.

"Joe don't like nobody running when he's hitting," Sparky explained.

It didn't bother me. If that's what they wanted, that's what I'd do, but it didn't make a whole lot of sense to me. I had just come off a season in which I led the American Association with 43 steals. Speed had always been a major part of my game, and I couldn't understand why they were taking that weapon away from me. I always felt that, given the green light, I could have been a 50-, 60-, 70-stolen-base guy. It was still part of my game, but after two years when Morgan was hitting behind me and they took that skill away from me, I lost the knack of stealing bases. I stole only nine bases in 1974, 16 in '75, and the most steals I ever had was 34 in 1976. In those three years, Morgan stole 58, 67, and 60 bases. Apparently it was all right for him to steal when Perez and Bench were at bat.

By July 31 we were nine and a half games up and on our way to the Reds' fourth National League pennant in seven years. By mid-August, with the division championship seemingly safely tucked away, I was consumed by being in the middle of a race for the National League batting championship with the defending champ Bill Madlock of the Chicago Cubs.

As August turned into September, we held a commanding lead over the Dodgers of eight and a half games with time rapidly running out on them. But the race for the batting title was getting interesting. I had been on Madlock's heels through most of the season, and on September 1 I was still within hailing distance of the league lead, .330 to Madlock's 338.

Eleven days later, I had dropped 14 points behind, .341 to .327, and it looked like I had blown it. But then I got hot, 5-for-10 against the Giants, 5-for-9 against the Dodgers, and I was back in the race at

.334 to Madlock's league-leading .345. Meanwhile, Garry Maddox of the Philadelphia Phillies had joined the party with a hot streak that pushed him ahead of me at .336. That was his high point, and he slowly dropped out of contention for the title.

Showing late foot, Pete Rose came on like a hard-charging thoroughbred pounding through the stretch and making his bid for the title. On September 24 he was well within reach of the lead at .330. Because he had been through this sort of thing before (he had already won three batting championships), and simply because he was Pete Rose who hated losing at tiddlywinks, his bid for the title had to be taken seriously. The next day, Pete fell off to .328 and then slowly slipped out of the race, but Madlock and I soldiered on.

An injury kept Madlock out of the lineup for five games in late September, and his absence was my chance to pick up some ground. On September 24 we began a West Coast trip with a three-game series against the Dodgers in Los Angeles. In the first game of the series, I got three hits. In the second game, I got two more hits and moved into a virtual tie for first place with Madlock, who was still on the injured list. He remained at .33598. I was at .33577.

Only five games remained, and I pressed my advantage. I got three more hits in the third game against the Dodgers (I was 8-for-13 in the three games) and raised my average to .339, while Madlock still had not returned to the lineup.

Our next stop was San Diego. I went 2-for-5, but officially I gained no ground, my average remaining at .339. With the Padres starting a pair of left-handers, Randy Jones and Brent Strom, in the last two games, Sparky kept me out of the lineup. So I went to the final three games of the season at home against the Atlanta Braves with a three-point lead over Madlock, who returned to the lineup against the Montreal Expos.

On October 1 I was 1-for-3 and Madlock was 1-for-4. I was batting .33931 to his .33531.

On October 2 I was hitless in three at-bats, and my average fell to .33750. Madlock also was hitless in three at-bats, and he was at .33333.

I took my .00417 lead into the final game of the season faced with a dilemma. Should I play or should I sit? I was getting a lot of advice from a lot of people, most of them well-meaning. But the more advice I got, the more confused I became. The opinions I got were pretty much right down the middle, with half the people saying play, the other half saying sit. My inclination was to play. I figured all I needed was one hit and I would clinch the batting title. Besides, I didn't want it on my résumé that I won a batting title by sitting rather than playing.

But in the end there was only one opinion that counted, and that belonged to Sparky Anderson. He said sit. I tried convincing him I should play, but it was no use. "I'm the manager of this team, not you," he said. "You're sitting!"

I like to think that Sparky made this decision because he truly believed that my chances of winning the batting title were better if I did not play. After all, Madlock had only one hit in seven at-bats since he returned to the lineup. What were the chances that he would be able to overtake me? Sparky said his only real chance of doing so was if I played and went 0-for-4.

I thought it was a mistake for such an issue to be made over whether I won a batting title or not, when we should have been thinking about and planning for playing in the National League Championship Series and, hopefully, the World Series.

I don't know what Sparky's real reason was for keeping me out of that final game. I never asked him, but it has always gnawed at me that he just didn't want me to win the batting title. Why? Possibly because I was a young player, and he didn't want me to get too much success too soon for fear that it would go to my head. Or maybe he didn't like the thought that I might be outshining his Big Four of

Bench, Rose, Morgan, and Perez. Am I being paranoid? Perhaps! So it's probably best that I just leave it that he believed he was doing what was best for my chances.

The starter for the Braves was Frank LaCorte, a right-hander in his first full season with a record of 3–11. I figured I could get to him for at least one hit, maybe more. But Sparky was adamant. He started Mike Lum, like me a left-handed hitter, in right field.

In Chicago the Cubs were taking on Montreal with veteran left-hander Woodie Fryman, a 13-game winner, pitching for the Expos. Madlock was batting third in the Cubs lineup.

Our publicity department had made contact with Wrigley Field and was monitoring what Madlock was doing.

In the first inning, Madlock beat out a bunt for a single.

In the third, he beat out an infield hit to third baseman Larry Parrish, who happened to be one of the best fielding third basemen in the game. Things were not going well for me. When word came down that Madlock had two hits in his first two at-bats, Sparky did an about-face and put me into the game in place of Dan Driessen. I got two at-bats, in the seventh and eighth, and I guess I was overanxious, because I struck out both times. Meanwhile, Madlock got two more hits, a 4-for-4 day, and left the game once his batting title was secured.

The final numbers were Madlock at .33852 and me at .33630.

I don't know if it would have made any difference, but I still say I should have started the game against the Braves.

I had to put aside the disappointment of missing out on winning the batting title (there would be other opportunities, I told myself) and concentrate on helping my team get back to the World Series. And just as we had in '75, we rolled to our second straight three-game sweep in the National League Championship Series, this time against the Philadelphia Phillies. The scores were 6–3, 6–2, and 7–6, and typically we used some late lightning in each game.

In Game 1 we were tied 1–1 when we scored two in the sixth and three in the eighth. In Game 2 we were down 2–0 and scored four in the sixth and two in the seventh. In Game 3 we were down 3–0 when we scored four in the seventh and three in the ninth.

Don Gullett starred in Game 1, both on the mound and at bat. He allowed just two hits and one run through eight innings and drove in half of our six runs. In Game 3 we were down 6–4 going into the bottom of the ninth, when Johnny Bench and George Foster hit home runs to tie it and I had the honor of driving in the series-winning run with a one-out single. For the series, I was 5-for-13, .385, and looking forward to going to the Big Apple for the World Series.

Under a feisty and battling new manager in Billy Martin and a blustery, hands-on new owner in George Steinbrenner (he had promised a championship in five years when he took over in 1973, and he had made good on his promise in four), the 1976 American League–champion New York Yankees had ended a 12-year drought and returned to their former glory days.

Although they were not yet the Bronx Zoo Yankees, they had their share of controversial characters like Mickey Rivers, Thurman Munson, Oscar Gamble, Lou Piniella, and Sparky Lyle. And they could also play some baseball. Munson was the team leader, a guy who played hard enough that he would have fit nicely as a member of the Big Red Machine. He even was from Ohio. He had batted .302, hit 17 homers, and drove in 105 runs. Graig Nettles was their big home-run hitter with 32, and they had thorough professionals like first baseman Chris Chambliss, second baseman Willie Randolph, left fielder Roy White, and an outstanding pitching staff headed up by Catfish Hunter, Ed Figueroa, and Dock Ellis, who combined for 53 wins, with Lyle and Dick Tidrow in the bullpen.

Nevertheless they were no match for the Big Red Machine, and we finished off our perfect postseason with a four-game sweep. I had a terrible Series, one hit in 17 at-bats (.059), but fortunately my bat wasn't needed. Bench batted .533, hit two home runs, drove in six runs, and was named World Series Most Valuable Player. George Foster hit .429, Davey Concepcion and Dan Driessen hit .357, Morgan hit .333, and Perez hit .313. For the Yankees, Munson was outstanding, batting .529.

And Sparky Anderson's mouth got him in trouble again. In the interview room after the fourth game, Sparky was at the podium heaping praise on Bench, which was deserved. But in doing so, he indirectly dissed Munson, which was not deserved.

"Let's don't embarrass nobody by comparing him to Johnny Bench," said Sparky, not realizing that Munson was standing in the back of the room waiting for his turn at the podium. Thurman never forgave Sparky for the slight, and who could blame him?

Even if I didn't do much at bat to help win the World Series, I still felt 1976 was a good year for me. I was especially proud of one fact: before George Foster and I got there, the Big Red Machine had never won a world championship; now they had won two in a row.

The clincher came in Yankee Stadium, a 7–2 win behind Gary Nolan and Will McEnaney and Johnny Bench hitting two home runs, good for five RBIs. Our starting lineup was Rose, 3b; Griffey, rf; Morgan, 2b; Perez, 1b; Driessen, dh; Foster, lf; Bench, c; Geronimo, cf; and Concepcion, ss. The date was October 21, 1976. It was the last time the "Great Eight" played together.

The next time they got together on a ballfield was 45 days short of 37 years later. On September 7, 2013, the Great Eight, considered by many as the greatest one-through-eight lineup of starting position players in baseball history, gathered at Great American Ballpark in Cincinnati on the occasion of the dedication of a statue of Joe Morgan.

I never had a close relationship with Morgan or any of the older guys when we were teammates. I was the young guy on the team, the new kid on the block, and I was beneath those guys. But times change and people mellow with the years.

Joe called me personally and asked me to come to the ceremony. I had just finished the season in Bakersfield on September 2, so I drove from California to my home in Florida and on the morning of the seventh, I flew from Florida to Cincinnati. We were all there, all eight of us, including Pete Rose. It was the first time Pete had been on the field in Cincinnati since he was suspended. Morgan arranged it. He's friendly with commissioner Bud Selig, and he asked the commissioner to approve him inviting Pete to the unveiling of his statue, and Selig said okay. That was it.

When Pete was introduced, he got this tremendous ovation that almost brought the house down, and when he walked onto the field, there were tears in Rose's eyes. I had never seen Pete cry before.

When I came up to the Reds, I stayed away from the big guys like Morgan, Bench, and Perez. Those older guys hardly interacted with us younger guys, but that was all right. I didn't mind it. I just enjoyed playing the game. I didn't need those guys to encourage me. Nobody had to encourage me. I was my own man. I looked at it this way: I had a job to do. I knew what I had to do to help the team win games. I was hitting between Pete Rose and Joe Morgan. If Pete got on base, I knew that he was the best guy in the world to go from first to third on a hit. I was the best guy to hit second because I could pull the ball in the hole better than anybody. Once I pulled the ball in the hole, Pete would be on third base. So Pete was on third and I was on first with nobody out. Next came Morgan, a good situational hitter. One year, 1976, he led the National League with 12 sacrifice flies.

That's why I was the best guy to hit second in that lineup. If Pete wasn't on base or Morgan didn't do his job and I was on first base, I could steal second and Perez or Bench or Foster could knock me in with a hit.

Bench would always tease me because I had three kids at such a young age and he had none. So what? I had kids. They're my kids. I never had anything against J.B. We just didn't have much to say to one another. But as people get older, they see things differently. Today J.B. is one of the best guys in the world. And he has kids of his own.

The Reds' Great Eight gets together just about every year at autograph shows. Maybe because I'm one of the older guys myself now, my relationship with those older guys is better than it was when we were players.

So dominant were the Reds in the early and mid-seventies, people were calling us a dynasty, expecting us to reel off three, four, five championships in a row. It never happened.

In 1977 we won only 88 games and finished 10 games behind the Dodgers despite acquiring one of the great pitchers of his era in a trade. On June 15 the Reds swung a much-heralded and controversial deal to land Tom Seaver from the New York Mets.

I had a great relationship with Seaver. I enjoyed playing with him. He was a fun guy with a weird sense of humor who liked to play practical jokes on his teammates. Besides, he was a great pitcher and one of the most competitive guys I've ever played with or against.

I remember facing him in the first game of the 1973 National League Championship Series. The first time I came up against him was in the second inning. One out, a runner on second base, and the first pitch Seaver threw to me hit me in the leg. When we became teammates, I asked Tom, "What were you thinking when you threw at me in the '73 playoffs?"

He said, "You weren't going to run."

Little did he know that Sparky had told me I wasn't allowed to run anyway.

Even though we didn't get him until midway in the season, Seaver won 14 games for us, and lost only three, on his way to 311 career victories and the Hall of Fame. But not even the great Tom Seaver or a huge breakout season from George Foster, who led the league with 52 homers and 149 runs batted in, could help us catch the Dodgers.

We improved in 1978 to win 92 games but finished two and a half games behind the Dodgers. Baseball still was without a wild-card format, so the Reds had gone two straight years without winning anything, and that was unacceptable to the people of Cincinnati, and especially to the Reds ownership, which had grown accustomed to winning.

After the 1978 season, we flew out for a series of games against teams in Japan. We spent a month in Japan and played 17 games there. Japanese baseball at the time had not progressed to the level it became a decade or two later, so the competition was not great. Of the 17 games, we won 14 and lost two, and one game ended in a tie. We traveled on the bullet train, which was outstanding. I really enjoyed that. The food—the Kobe steaks and the lobster—was great, and the hotels we stayed in were first class, except in some places the beds were too small. It was a great experience, but weird. First there was the trip, which seemed like it would never end. We left from Cincinnati and flew to Anchorage, Alaska, and then from Anchorage to Japan. With the time change and all, by the time we got to Japan we were whipped. It took us a day or two to shake the jet lag and get acclimated to the time change.

Also most of our players brought their wives, and back then women were not allowed to go to the ballpark in Japan. So the wives were never permitted to come to the games. Instead, they were taken on tours around the country and entertained elsewhere, so we didn't see them for about two weeks while we were playing games in every little city in the country. We played in front of capacity crowds and were well received by the fans. We flew to Sapporo, which is way up north and was the coldest place we played. Sapporo was where they held the 1972 Winter Olympics. From our dugout we could see the ski lifts in the Olympic Stadium up in the mountains.

We got to play several games against the great Japanese home-run champion Sadaharu Oh, who had that unusual hitting style. A left-handed hitter, Oh would lift his right leg before he swung as a timing mechanism, because most of the pitchers in Japan hesitated before they delivered the ball to the plate—some of the Japanese pitchers in the United States today still do. That could mess up your timing, so Oh came up with his timing device. I could understand why he did. Hitting against some of the Japanese pitchers, I often had to slow things down to hit. They had one pitcher, kind of the Rawly Eastwick of Japan, a closer they called "Spiderman" who would wind up and then stop. He'd get ready to throw, and he'd stop again. He might stop two or three times before he threw the ball. By then you were thinking, *When is he going to release it?* It kept us off balance, which was their intention. It took me a little while to understand what pitchers that hesitated before they threw were doing. I felt I had to do something to get my timing down. What I did was, I never even watched them; I just looked for the baseball.

The thing about Sadaharu Oh was that as great a hitter as he was, I don't think he had ever seen a good sinkerball. We had guys like Tommy Hume, Mike LaCoss, Clay Carroll, Pedro Borbon, all with excellent hard sinkers, and they just ate him alive. He couldn't lift that sinker and hit it over the fence. The first game we played, Tom Seaver pitched, and Sadaharu Oh was hitless in his first two or three at-bats until Seaver threw him a fastball and he hit it over the fence. It made him look like the big guy in Japanese baseball, which he was, and the crowd went wild. I figured Tom knew all that and was just being a friendly opponent by giving Oh a fastball he could handle.

Oh was a first baseman, and he almost got me killed in one game. I hit a ground ball to the second baseman. I beat it out, and as I crossed first base Oh missed the throw from the second baseman and it hit me right in the forehead. Oh was all apologetic, bowing and scraping for missing the ball and almost causing me to get hurt.

The strangest thing about the Japan trip was that Dick Wagner, the Reds general manager, went around asking the players questions about Sparky Anderson. A lot of the guys were uncomfortable with that. It made us wonder if maybe something was up with Sparky, but no, it couldn't be. We figured Sparky was all set to be our manager in 1979, maybe forever.

On November 28, six days after we returned from Japan, we were hit by stunning news. Reds general manager Dick Wagner informed Sparky Anderson—who had averaged 96 wins a season and won five division titles, four National League pennants, and two World Series as the Reds' manager—that he would not be back in 1979. Rather than deliver the news over the telephone, Wagner flew out to California and called Sparky at his home in Thousand Oaks, California, and asked him to come to Wagner's hotel. Sparky probably figured Wagner was there to discuss possible trades for the 1979 season, or perhaps even offer Sparky a contract extension. Instead, he dropped his hammer.

No official reason was given for removing Sparky as manager—although failing to finish first for two straight years was reason enough for the decision and would serve as a legitimate explanation for such a drastic and unpopular move—but there were all sorts of rumors going around. Some said that management felt Sparky was too soft, not as much of a disciplinarian as they would have liked. But how are you going to discipline Pete Rose, Johnny Bench, Joe Morgan, and Tony Perez?

Others pointed out that in his nine years with the Reds, Sparky had acquired a great deal of clout and reasoned the front office may have been upset that he had usurped their authority. In order to shoot Sparky down and regain its power, management ordered Sparky to get rid of a couple of his coaches. When Sparky refused, that's when they dropped the ax on him. In Sparky's defense, for his stand with his coaches he gets high marks for loyalty.

As shocking as was the announcement in 1970 that the Cincinnati Reds had hired Sparky Anderson as their manager, this news that he would not be back as manager was even more shocking.

SPARKY

Maybe my perception of Sparky's treatment of me, and others, was all wrong. Maybe there was nothing personal in it at all. Maybe it was simply Sparky being Sparky.

LETTING SPARKY ANDERSON GO WAS AN INDICATION THAT the Reds were about to break up that old gang of theirs, the Big Red Machine, and—as they like to say in baseball—"go in a different direction."

The dismantling actually began on December 16, 1976, when the Reds traded Tony Perez and Will McEnaney to the Montreal Expos for Woodie Fryman and Dale Murray. Perez was traded to make room for Danny Driessen at first base. It was a mistake and an injustice to Driessen. Sparky hardly played him. For four years he mostly sat and now he was being asked to replace a star and a future Hall of Famer. It wasn't fair to Danny. He simply was not ready for such a huge task.

To make matters worse, Perez still had a lot of good baseball left in him. He would play another 10 seasons (including the last three of his career as a part-time player back with the Reds, which seemed like sort of a mea culpa for trading him), hit 102 homers, and drive in 537 runs. In his first four seasons after he left Cincinnati, Doggie hit 71 homers and drove in 347 runs. The Reds certainly could have used that kind of production. Had they not traded him, it's conceivable we could have won four straight World Series, maybe more.

The shocking news of Anderson's abrupt firing left me with mixed emotions. On the one hand, I had tremendous respect for Sparky, and I was concerned that we would miss his leadership, his experience, and his résumé of success. On the other hand I was puzzled by some of the things Sparky had done, or not done, with me. I felt like the young man who, grown up and matured, leaves home and hearth, cuts the apron strings, and steps out on his own. Under Sparky, I felt that every move I made was being orchestrated by him. His departure was my chance to be my own man.

I never had any real problem with Sparky—no blowout, no confrontation, no harsh words with him. As a matter of fact, I rarely had *any* words with him at all. Maybe I should take that as a compliment, an indication that I was not high maintenance. We all crave attention, affection, and a pat on the back when we do something good, but Sparky was not very free with pats on the back. At least not with me, he wasn't.

There was not one incident in particular that bothered me, rather a series of little slights. Maybe I was being paranoid, insecure, and overly sensitive, but all of the small offenses he made against me that I've detailed thus far rubbed me the wrong way.

Individually, none of those things were so terrible—they were even explainable—but strung together they formed a disturbing pattern. I'm fairly certain that if you talked to guys like Davey Concepcion, George Foster, Danny Driessen, Doug Flynn, John Vukovich, Cesar Geronimo, and Ed Armbrister, they'd tell you the same thing: Sparky never spent a lot of time talking with them either. Part of the reason was that Sparky was spending a lot of his time with the writers, and the other part was that he was spending a lot of his time with the Reds' so-called Big Four—Bench, Rose, Morgan, and Perez—so there wasn't enough time left over for the "little people."

It seemed that Sparky only bragged on four players. They were the only ones he talked about. It was as if the rest of the team didn't exist. His Big Four was more important to Sparky than anything else, because when he first got to Cincinnati, Johnny Bench had told him, "You just sit there, don't say anything, and we'll make you a star." And they did.

I once heard that Sparky admitted he never treated all his players as equals, and he rationalized it by saying that any player who produced like Bench, Rose, Perez, and Morgan produced would also get preferential treatment. Those four were the center of Sparky's universe. The rest of us were satellites.

For a while, Sparky put Don Gullett on the same pedestal as the Big Four, but then after the 1976 season Gullett made the mistake of asking for a guaranteed two-year contract for $200,000, and from that moment, Gullett was no longer one of Sparky's fair-haired boys. There was no such thing as a guaranteed contract in those days, and even multiple-year contracts were rare. All of a sudden Sparky stopped talking about Gullett, and the Reds let Gullett go.

Gullett signed as a free agent with the Yankees. One of the reasons the Reds let him go was that because of the strain he was putting on his shoulder with his delivery, they feared he was susceptible to injury. Sure enough, after Gullett was 14–4 for the Yankees in 1977, he was 4–2 the next season when he hurt his arm, and he never pitched again.

I never could figure out if Sparky liked me or not. If I had to guess, I'd say that what Sparky thought about me was that I was probably one of the strongest players that he had, that I could handle almost anything. He moved me around in the batting order, and I always played well for him and never complained about how I was treated. I always figured there was a reason he was doing certain things. I don't know if it was because he didn't like me, if he felt I was in competition with his Big Four, or if I was too young to be doing what I was doing as a player. I didn't understand why he was so cool toward me. I never said anything about what was going on. I never talked to the press about it. I never said anything bad about Sparky Anderson, and I always played hard.

The first four games I played for him, I had two hits in three of the games and three hits in the other. After eight games I had 16 hits and was batting .533, so I had to have made a good first impression on him.

I was the youngest player on that team. I was nine years younger than Pete, six years younger than Joe, eight years younger than Doggie, two years younger than J.B., two years younger than

Davey, two years younger than Geronimo, and a year younger than Foster. And it seemed like Sparky, for whatever reason, did not want the youngest to shine. Maybe he just wanted to keep us humble.

Sparky hardly said a word to me for 20 years. I guess I should take that as a compliment, that I didn't need to be motivated to play hard. The record will show that I produced for him and that I never said anything nasty about him.

All I can do is tell my story about what happened. I'm not trying to ridicule Sparky, because I respect the man. He was the manager, and he had to manage some of the biggest egos in the history of the game.

Maybe my perception of Sparky's treatment of me, and others, was all wrong. Maybe there was nothing personal in it at all. Maybe it was simply Sparky being Sparky.

The last time I saw Sparky I thought there was something wrong with him. He seemed to be lacking his old "spark." He was shaking quite a bit and not making a lot of sense when he spoke. Later it came out that the shaking was the result of Parkinson's disease and that he was in the early stages of dementia. Sadly, he passed away in 2010, much too early, at the age of 76.

To replace Anderson as manager, the Reds selected John McNamara, who had managed the Oakland Athletics and San Diego Padres with only moderate success. He was presumably chosen to manage the Reds because he had a reputation for being a disciplinarian (one of the criticisms of Sparky was that he was too soft on discipline).

If McNamara was a disciplinarian, I never saw it. I got along with him very well. I enjoyed playing for him. He was much different as a manager than Sparky. At first, his main concern was coming in and replacing a man who had been so successful and was such a fan favorite. Also he was taking over a team that was missing some of its pieces. Perez was gone. Rose was gone. Only Bench and Morgan remained from the Big Four, so besides those two, Mac relied on the younger players who were by that point the veterans on the team, like George Foster, Davey Concepcion, Danny Driessen, and me.

With Rose gone, McNamara batted me in the leadoff spot, and I was having a pretty good season when, on June 13, playing against the Mets in Shea Stadium, I led off the game with a double down the left-field line. Steve Henderson was in left field. I rounded second base thinking I could stretch my double into a triple, but you never want to make the first out at third base, so when I saw Henderson come up with the ball, I stopped and headed back to second. I pivoted, turned, and headed back, and my spikes got caught. I could feel something pop in my knee. I was taken out of the game and replaced by Dave Collins.

By the time they got me into the dugout, my knee was swollen to three times its normal size. The Mets doctor looked at it and said he thought I had a torn cartilage. They weren't taking injured players to the hospital in those days, and the Reds wanted to wait until we got home and they could send me to our team doctor.

I missed three days and was back in the lineup on June 17. I was in terrible pain, but I continued to play. To get through the pain, I was popping Darvons like they were M&Ms. I played with the pain for six weeks, and I finally had to stop taking the Darvon because I was hallucinating, but without the Darvon the pain was unbearable.

On August 8 we were at home playing the third game of a three-game series against the Atlanta Braves. Phil Niekro was scheduled to start for the Braves. I seemed to always have success against Niekro and his knuckleball, mainly because I had a short swing. Earlier in the year, I had hit a home run against him. Niekro knew I hit him well, and he had watched me in the first two games of the series and noticed that I could hardly walk, let alone run. That took away one of my weapons, the ability to steal bases, so in my first two times at bat, Niekro walked me.

By that time the pain was so severe I told McNamara, "Mac, I can't play anymore like this; I'm in too much pain."

He said, "You tell me what you want to do."

John gave me the option of continuing to play or taking care of my knee, which I appreciated. He was treating me like a veteran, and that's why I liked John McNamara. I had to find out exactly what was wrong with my knee. Everybody kept telling me it was torn cartilage, but the Reds trainer, Larry Starr, didn't agree, and neither did I. Larry's assistant told me he could get me an appointment with Dr. Warren Harding, the head of orthopedics at the University of Cincinnati Hospital.

I arranged to see Dr. Harding, and he confirmed that it was not a torn ligament or cartilage. At the time, they were just getting into arthroscopy, where they would stick a needle and a camera into the area and scope it out. That's what they did about a week later, and what they discovered was that when I caught my spikes at Shea Stadium, I had snapped a piece of bone about the size of a 50¢ piece off the back of my knee that had crumbled up in the knee.

Dr. Harding said he was amazed that I was able to play with that piece of bone grinding in on my knee and with bone fragments flying around in my kneecap. I had not only played with it for six weeks, but when I got hurt I was batting .287 and after playing six weeks with the pain my average had risen to .316, which would have been good for fourth place in the National League if I had enough at-bats to qualify for the batting title, which I didn't.

I had to go to California to Dr. Frank Jobe, the pioneer and inventor of Tommy John surgery, and he operated on me on August 14, just six days after I took myself out of the game against the Atlanta Braves. Dr. Jobe opened my knee, looked in, and cleaned it out. He discovered that I had no cartilage in the knee, so he drilled two or three holes in my femur to generate cartilage. I wasn't allowed to walk on that leg for another six weeks, which took me to the end of the season.

With McNamara at the helm, and me playing only 95 games, we won 90 games and won the National League West title by a game and a half over the Houston Astros. George Foster was our big bomber with 30 home runs and 98 RBIs,.

My injury kept me out of the National League Championship Series and I had to look on helplessly as we were swept in three games by the Pittsburgh Pirates, the team made famous as the "We Are Family" Pirates.

The Reds' defections continued the following year when a month before the start of spring training, Joe Morgan signed a free-agent contract with the Houston Astros, the team with which he broke into the big leagues 17 years before. To add to the confusion, there was unrest that spring on the labor front and strong rumors that a strike halting the start of the season was inevitable. At the same time, I heard from one of the writers covering the Reds that there were rumors of a possible trade involving me. My source said the Reds were in talks with the New York Mets and had agreed on a deal in principle that would send me to New York in exchange for a young pitcher named Craig Swan, who was coming off a season in which he won 14 games for a last-place team.

As it turned out, when the strike was averted, the deal fell through, saving me from ending up with what, at the time, was a bad team.

I was healthy and ready to go in 1980, and pleased when John McNamara said he was moving me down to the No. 2 hole in the batting order, a spot I was more familiar with. The reason for the move, John said, was that he wanted to put Dave Collins in the leadoff spot to take advantage of his speed, and he thought I was the best guy to hit behind Collins because I was a selective hitter. He tried a couple of other guys in the No. 2 hole, but they told John that they couldn't hit behind Collins because Davey would tell them when he was going to steal, and when he didn't steal, they were confused and didn't know what to swing at.

What I did was tell Davey if I got a good pitch to hit I was swinging even if I knew he was running. I told him that early in the game I'd give him his stolen base. But I said that late in the game, if situations came up and I got a good pitch to hit, a pitch I knew I could hit, I was going to drive it somewhere. And he understood. We worked well together. He stole 79 bases that year, third in the National League, and he scored 94 runs. Healthy again, I played in 146 games, batted .294, hit 13 homers, drove in 85 runs, and was named to my third All-Star team.

I was told it came down to me and Dusty Baker for the final spot on the All-Star team, and Chuck Tanner, the manager of the Pittsburgh Pirates, had the last call and he chose me over Dusty. That didn't go over very well in Los Angeles, where the game was played. Dusty was a Dodger and a fan favorite, so I was booed whenever I was introduced or came to bat.

I got into a scoreless game in the fourth inning as a replacement for Dave Kingman. The American League had scored two runs in the top of the fifth when I came to bat for the first time in the bottom of the inning and belted a long home run into the seats in right-center field off Tommy John. Later I singled in the seventh and flew out in the eighth. We won the game 4–2, and I was voted the game's Most Valuable Player.

Although we won only one fewer game in 1980 than we had in '79, we slipped a notch and finished third in the NL West behind the Astros and Dodgers.

The 1981 baseball season was a weird one, with Major League Baseball's fourth work stoppage since 1972. The issue was free-agent compensation, in other words, what a team would get in return if one of its players left as a free agent and signed with another team. Play was stopped on June 12, and it resumed on August 9. In the

50-day work stoppage 713 games, or 38 percent of the season, were lost, plus $146 million in players' salaries and owners' revenue.

Once the strike was settled and the schedule could resume, the major remaining issue was owners and players coming to agreement on how the championships of each division and each league would be determined.

What they decided was that the season would be played in a split-season format. All games that had been played up to June 12, the date of the work stoppage, would constitute the first half. The second half would be the remaining schedule, starting from the resumption of play on August 10 until the end of the season. The winners of the first half and the winners of the second half in each league would meet in a best-of-five playoff series to determine the league champions, who would then square off in the World Series. Should the same team finish in first place in both halves, then a wild-card team would provide the opposition in the playoff for the league championship.

As luck would have it, the Reds finished in second place in the first half, a half game behind the Dodgers, and in second place in the second half, a game and a half behind the Astros, and had nothing to show for it. It didn't matter that our overall record of 66–42 was the best in the National League, four games better than the Dodgers and six games better than Houston—in fact, it was the best record in the major leagues. We were on the outside looking in as the Dodgers beat the Astros for the NL West title, then beat the Expos for the National League pennant and beat the Yankees in the World Series.

I had another good year, fifth in the league with 123 hits and sixth in the league with a .311 batting average (I had hit higher than .300 in six of my nine major league seasons or parts).

By 1982 free agency was an established fact in Major League Baseball. Player after player, many who didn't have the statistical résumé, the experience, the World Series rings, or the record of success I had were signing long-term contracts for seven figures. Meanwhile I had just completed a three-year contract worth $500,000, or $166,667 per year. While it was good money, more than I ever dreamed I would make when I was a kid back in Donora, it still was well below the going rate for a major league veteran with eight years in the big leagues. I figured it was time I got my piece of the rock.

Although I was eligible for free agency, I knew there was no way the Reds were going to pay me the going rate for a player with my history. The Reds wanted to trade me to make certain they wouldn't lose me without getting something in return. They said they would trade me to the American League, and I told them the New York Yankees were the only American League team I would go to.

My agent at the time, Tom Reich (coincidentally pronounced "Rich") was pretty close to Yankees owner George Steinbrenner, who had signed several of Tom's clients. Reich arranged a meeting with the three of us—Steinbrenner, Reich, and me—and we talked about the parameters of a contract. The Yankees had just lost the 1981 World Series to the Los Angeles Dodgers but still had a powerful team with Reggie Jackson and Dave Winfield, so they looked like a good bet to reach the World Series again. I could have signed with them as a free agent, but I wanted the Reds to get something in return, so we gave them 72 hours to make a deal. If the Reds and Yankees couldn't come to an agreement on a trade, I would sign with the Yankees as a free agent and the Reds would end up with nothing.

On November 4, 1981, the Yankees and Reds completed a trade that was attached to a provision that I sign a long-term contract with the Yankees as a free agent. The Reds would send me to the Yankees in exchange for two pitchers: Brian Ryder, who never spent a day in the major leagues, and a player to be named later that turned out to be Freddie Toliver, who pitched in seven seasons for Cincinnati,

Philadelphia, Minnesota, San Diego, and Pittsburgh with a record of 10–16. Six weeks later, the Yankees also signed Dave Collins as a free agent.

The Reds were willing to cut ties with me because they were looking to get younger and because they were told by their medical staff that with the shape my knee was in, I wasn't going to be able to play much longer. And they also got two young pitchers in return. For me, the trade meant that I'd be going to a team that had shown its willingness to pony up big dollars for free agents. So it looked like a win-win all around.

With the Yankees, I signed a six-year contract worth $6.25 million, more money than I ever knew there was in the world.

I was on my way to Easy Street.

To New York…

To the Yankees…

To the Big Apple…

To the Bronx Zoo…

To "the Boss," George Steinbrenner…

And to revolving-door managers.

BILLYBALL

It didn't take long for me to realize that when I joined the Yankees I was entering the Land of Oz.

TO SAY THAT GOING FROM THE CONSISTENCY AND continuity of the Cincinnati Reds to the constant upheaval of the New York Yankees, from laid-back Cincinnati to the city that never sleeps, from beautiful Ohio to frenetic New York City, from conservative Reds president Bob Howsam to meddlesome, impetuous Yankees owner George Steinbrenner was a culture shock is putting it mildly.

In Cincinnati, I played for one manager in the first six years of my major league career.

With the Yankees, my first manager, Hall of Fame pitcher Bob Lemon, lasted 14 games.

In Cincinnati, I had two managers in nine years.

With the Yankees, I had six managers in five seasons, including Billy Martin twice.

Players came and players went. Coaches came and coaches went. Managers came and managers went…and then they came back again.

The Yankees, the most successful franchise in baseball history, had gone nine years without winning a championship when George Steinbrenner—a shipbuilder from Ohio, of all places—headed up a group that purchased the team from the Columbia Broadcasting System. Steinbrenner promised Yankees fans he would give them a championship in five years. He did it in four. He spent wildly on free agents (Reggie Jackson, Catfish Hunter, Don Gullett, Rich "Goose" Gossage, Dave Winfield) to win the World Series in 1977 and 1978 and another American League pennant in 1981, just before another dry spell hit.

Before I agreed to the trade to the Yankees and signed a long-term contract, I needed some assurances. I soon discovered that

George Steinbrenner was a charmer, someone who would tell you whatever you wanted to hear and who could be very persuasive. He was also a big spender. He took Tom Reich and me to dinner in New York, and I told Steinbrenner that the only way I would sign with the Yankees was if they re-signed Reggie Jackson. George said, "Okay. We're going to sign Reggie, and that means you'll hit second and play right field and Reggie will bat fourth and DH." That was the plan. The lineup would be Willie Randolph leading off, me second, Dave Winfield third, Reggie fourth, and then Nettles and whoever. That's the way it was supposed to be. It sounded like a winner to me. I was convinced. A few days after that dinner, on January 22, 1982, Reggie Jackson signed as a free agent with the California Angels. George flat-out didn't tell the truth, which was his forte.

Soon after I signed with the Yankees, I got a call from a reporter who asked me how many home runs I was going to hit in Yankee Stadium. Was I going to hit 40 home runs?

I said I hadn't hit 40 home runs in three years. I pointed out that Davey Collins and I together had never hit as many as 20 home runs in a season. In 1980, the last non-strike year, we had hit only 16 home runs combined.

There's no doubt this was all coming from Steinbrenner. What was he thinking? He was trying to get the press to think of me as the guy who was going to fill the vacancy left by Jackson, who had hit 41 home runs in the last non-strike season. George wanted me to be like Oscar Gamble, just pull everything and pop home runs into Yankee Stadium's short porch in right field. But that wasn't my style.

It didn't take long for me to realize that when I joined the Yankees I was entering the Land of Oz. I reported to Fort Lauderdale for my first spring training as a Yankee about five or 10 pounds over my playing weight, something I rarely did. But I had had a busy off-season. I was still having trouble with my knee, so I wasn't able to get the weight off. I figured I'd do that in spring training.

My legs weren't ready for the first week of spring training, which involved a lot of running. I had developed some swelling in the knee that had to be drained about four times, and George was alarmed. He didn't want anybody to see me, so he sent orders not to have me work out on the main field at Fort Lauderdale Stadium but to take me out of sight behind the left-field fence and have me work out on the backfield.

I wasn't allowed to take batting practice on the main field. Even when I was starting the exhibition game, I would take batting practice on the backfield with the young kids while the other starters took batting practice on the main field because George didn't want anyone to see me limping.

I didn't mind. I understood what he was thinking. He had just made a trade for me, and if the writers saw me hobbling around, unable to run at top speed, and wrote about it, that would make George look bad.

My contract with the Yankees had a clause that I was never told about that stated if my knee gave out Steinbrenner wouldn't have to pay me. (I never would have agreed to such a clause, but it was done without my approval. I admit I should have read the contract more carefully, but I didn't). So to test my knee and force the issue, Bob Lemon was told to play me every day in spring training, which he did. I played almost every exhibition game in Florida, home and away, getting three or four at-bats a game. I wound up with about 111 at-bats.

The 1982 Yankees team I joined was not the one I signed up for. Not only was Reggie Jackson gone, the team was being constructed on the fly, undergoing changes to the point that the team that finished the season hardly resembled the team that started the season.

Davey Collins, a free agent, and I were the new kids on the block, but before we had even played a game in the regular season, we had seniority.

Doyle Alexander came in a trade on March 30.

Shane Rawley arrived two days later. April fool!

Roy Smalley came in a trade on April 10.

Bob Lemon, a guy I liked a lot but hardly got to know, was fired on April 26 and was replaced by Gene Michael, who managed 86 games and was replaced by Clyde King.

John Mayberry came in a trade on May 5.

Butch Wynegar joined us on May 12.

Concessionaires could have boosted sales by coming to the clubhouse and hawking scorecards complete with names and numbers.

Once the season started, I had very little contact with George Steinbrenner, but I do remember one incident when Gene "Stick" Michael was the manager. Steinbrenner and Michael were very close. Stick was the one guy who could, or would, exchange barbs with the Boss, who was always getting on players for not catching a ball or making a mistake. One day Michael said, "You think it's that easy, George? Why don't you come down on the field and catch some?"

George took Stick at his word. "Yeah," he said, "I'll come down."

At the time, Steinbrenner had us all wearing blue jogging suits, which were the worst things in the world. They gave off an odor that was awful. We'd take shower after shower, and we couldn't get rid of the smell.

George came down on the field in his blue jogging suit and took his position at third base, and Gene started hitting him ground balls. Picture a two-year-old kid. A ball is hit to him, and he doesn't get his glove down until the ball is past him. That was George.

I said "Stick, you better not hit him any ball harder than that, because you're going to kill him."

He said, "Watch this next one."

Stick hit another one, but he made sure not to hit it right at George. He hit it to George's right, and by the time he put his glove down the ball was already down the left-field line. He had no chance to catch it. None! And that ended the fungo session.

I never had a problem with George. He treated me okay and generally left me alone, but he did get on me one time for something that wasn't my fault. I was playing left field, and Rickey Henderson was playing center field. A ball was hit between us, and Rickey ran it down. When he went to throw it into the infield it slipped out of his hand, and he threw it backward. I was backing him up, and the ball sailed right past me. I ducked, and Rickey started laughing. I wound up picking up the ball and throwing it to the cutoff man.

After the game Yogi Berra came to me.

"Hey, you gotta come in early tomorrow and catch some ground balls in the outfield."

"For what?"

"George wants you to field grounders because you threw that ball back to the wall."

"It wasn't me. It was Rickey that threw that ball. I was just backing him up."

"George wants you to do that because he can't tell Rickey."

Another time, and this had nothing to do with me, we were in Detroit and we were scheduled to leave after a night game for a flight to Baltimore. We got to the airport, and our traveling secretary, Bill "Killer" Kane, couldn't find the flight. We rode around looking for our plane and couldn't find it, so evidently Killer called Steinbrenner, who told him not to find the flight until George called him.

Steinbrenner managed to learn the location of the missing plane, and we boarded at about 3:00 AM. They loaded the equipment and our luggage on the plane, taxied for takeoff, then we had an hour and a half flight to Baltimore and another 45-minute-to-an-hour bus ride to the hotel, and we didn't get settled into our rooms until about 7:00 AM. We had a doubleheader scheduled to start at 5:30 PM. Because there was some ceremony going on prior to the start of the doubleheader, in order to get in our work, players had to get to the ballpark in the early afternoon, and most of us went without any sleep.

Another time we had a day off on the schedule. My kids were living with their mother in Cincinnati, but it had been two years since I was able to get there. I figured the day off would be a perfect opportunity to fly to Cincinnati, see my kids, get over to watch Junior play his high school game, spend the night, and fly back to New York in time for our game the following night. I got up early in the morning and flew to Cincinnati. When I got off the plane my wife said there had been a telephone call from the Yankees saying that George had ordered a workout that afternoon and I had to be back in New York. I had to skip Junior's game and get back on a plane at 11:00 AM and fly to New York. I took a taxi to Yankee Stadium and found out that the workout had been canceled.

That was the sort of stuff that went on regularly in the Bronx Zoo.

In my first season as a Yankee, we finished in fifth place in a seven-team division with a record of 79–83. My .277 average, 12 home runs, 54 RBIs, and 10 stolen bases neither pushed my new team to greater heights nor was the reason for its failure.

After that abomination of a season, George Steinbrenner did what George Steinbrenner always did when his team didn't live up to his overly ambitious expectations: he signed free agents (Don Baylor, Steve Kemp, and Bob Shirley) and brought back Billy Martin to manage, that time for his third hitch.

At the end of the 1982 season, Yogi Berra, who was one of the coaches, told me, "Don't bring your outfield glove to spring training, bring a first baseman's glove, because next year you're going to play first." (During the season the Yankees had used eight different first basemen—Steve Balboni, Dave Collins, Butch Hobson, Don Mattingly, John Mayberry, Lee Mazzilli, Dave Revering, and Bob Watson).

I said, "Okay, I have one."

When I got to spring training Yogi said, "Don't worry about your first baseman's glove; you're not going to play first."

"I thought you said I was going to play first," I said.

"No, no, no," he said. "You're going to platoon in center field with Jerry Mumphrey."

"Mumphrey?" I said. "He's a switch-hitter."

"You're still going to platoon in center field," he answered.

In spring training they tried about 11 different guys at first base, and not one of them satisfied Steinbrenner. The day we were scheduled to break camp and go to New Orleans to play three exhibition games, Billy Martin told Yogi to tell me to get my first baseman's mitt and that I would be playing first.

"Yogi," I said, "I haven't taken ground balls at first base all spring. I don't have any idea what's going on. The last time I played first base was in Little League or high school."

"Billy wants you at first base," he said.

When the season started, they moved me all around. I played first base from April 5 to 10, center field and left field from April 12 to 14, back to first base from April 15 to June 1, center field on June 2 and 3, first base on June 4 and 5, center field from June 6 to 13, and first base from June 14 to 19.

The turning point came one day when I was playing first and a ball was hit in the third base–shortstop hole. Roy Smalley ranged far to his right, backhanded it, straightened up, and fired to first. The throw took a short hop, I picked it, and the umpire called the runner out. That did it! From that day on I was the first baseman for the New York Yankees. Wally Pipp. Lou Gehrig. Moose Skowron. Chris Chambliss. And me.

During that season, Don Mattingly was riding the shuttle between Columbus, the Yankees' top farm team, and New York. He came up to stay at the end of June and played first base until August 6, when they put him back in the outfield and I moved back to first base for the remainder of the season.

I told Billy Martin, "Mattingly's not an outfielder and he's a terrific first baseman, why don't you put him at first and put me in the outfield. Isn't that logical?"

I thought that made sense. It would have been the perfect scenario to give Mattingly playing time and experience at first base and give the Yankees a chance to see him play the bag. After all, they were grooming him to be their first baseman of the future. It also would have helped the defense, because there was no doubt Donnie was a better first baseman than me and I was a better outfielder than him.

But there was no logic and nothing made sense in the Bronx Zoo, so Mattingly stayed in the outfield and I remained the first baseman. I played in 101 games at first base that season and had a fielding percentage of .992. Not bad. And I had one of my better seasons with the bat, a .306 average, 11 home runs, and 46 runs batted in playing about 70 percent of the time, surprising because Billy Martin and I were like oil and water. Billy had his issues and a lifestyle and personality I didn't always admire, so we never really hit it off. I'll get into the reasons later, but for now I have to give the devil his due. As a manager, Billy Martin to me at the time was one of the best in baseball. And that includes the managers in the National League. I soon learned what it was that had made him so successful and sought after as a manager.

Believe it or not, I really liked playing for Billy Martin. He understood how to manufacture runs, and he could manufacture runs even if he didn't have a good team. To me, he was more like a National League manager than an American League manager—bunting, stealing bases, playing hit and run...all the things that made the National League style of play what it was.

He was unbelievable at running a game. He always seemed to be two or three steps ahead of the guy in the other dugout. He was daring and creative. He thought of things that most managers would never think of. And he instilled in his players the fighting spirit that was his personal trademark. If you played hard for him, he played you and he had your back. If you didn't play hard, you sat. I believe I always played hard no matter who the manager was, so even if Billy didn't like me, he played me.

From a team that had won 79 games and finished fifth 16 games out of first place the year before, we improved to 91–72 and finished third, only seven games behind the leader.

Despite his brilliance at running a game, which I admired and respected, I can't put Billy Martin at the top of my list of managers I've played for or baseball people I've known. From the time he returned as manager of the Yankees in 1983, I had the feeling he resented me. I felt about Billy Martin about the same as I felt about Sparky Anderson. I respected them both, but I was confused by them both as well. Martin, like Sparky, rarely spoke to me and didn't seem to like me. We never had words or anything, but I felt uncomfortable around him.

When I took the time and trouble to think about why he was so cool toward me, I came to the conclusion that it was because of the 1976 World Series when my Cincinnati Reds swept his New York Yankees in four games. What did that have to do with me? Nothing really; I had one hit in 17 at-bats in that series, a .059 average. The Reds could have swept them without me.

I came to realize that Martin just was not a good loser. He took losing personally, as if it was an indictment of him as a manager. In that 1976 World Series Sparky Anderson got on Martin's raw nerve. Every move Sparky made worked, and every move Billy made backfired, and you could see that Billy was burning. There were times I thought he and Sparky might come to blows.

So when I became a Yankee and Martin returned as manager, I was a constant reminder to him of that '76 World Series, the symbol of what was Billy's greatest failure. He took it out on me because I was the only member of that '76 team who was on his team in 1983. It became obvious to me that seven years after the fact, Billy still had not gotten over the embarrassment of that defeat, and he never would. He said flat-out many times that he didn't like National League players.

That was back in the days when players rarely changed leagues, back before free agency and interleague trading. At the time, the American and National Leagues had separate presidents, used different umpires, and even played by different rules (the designated hitter). Players took pride in their league. Billy came from a time when the rivalry between the two leagues was so fierce players from one league treated players in the other league like the hated enemy; you didn't just want to beat them in the All-Star Game, you wanted to annihilate them (see Pete Rose vs. Ray Fosse in the 1970 All-Star Game).

I felt that every opportunity Billy had, he tried to embarrass me. He might bat me fourth one day and then bat me ninth the next day. When the writers asked him about it, Billy said, "We need two leadoff men [because of the designated hitter, managers often used a 'second leadoff man' in the nine hole of their lineup.]"

I will say on Martin's behalf that whatever he felt about me, the Cincinnati Reds, or the 1976 World Series, he played me. And I produced for him. In my four full years with the Yankees, my highest average was .306 in 1983 and the most RBIs I had were 69 in 1985, both years when Martin was the manager. I don't know if that's a tribute to Martin or to me.

Where I had the biggest problem with Martin was when he decided to take things out on my kids. From time to time, my two sons, Ken Jr. and Craig, came to New York to spend time with me, and I'd take them with me to the ballpark and send them to the batting cages, where they could play.

One day the assistant clubhouse man, Nick Priore, came to me and said, "Somebody told me to tell you to tell your two kids to be quiet."

There were other players' kids down by the cages. Piniella's kids were there, and Nettles kids, and I don't know who else's. They'd go there every night. Their mothers would let them go there because it was out of the way of everybody and they could play. And kids being kids, they made a little too much noise. They all did. But my two boys were the only ones that were singled out.

I said to Priore, "You tell whoever told you to tell me that to come and tell me that to my face. Who told you to tell me that?"

"I can't tell you," Nick said.

But I already knew who it was. I made a point of talking to Priore in a voice loud enough to be heard in the manager's office, if you get my meaning. I was getting so steamed that coach Jeff Torborg had to hold me back.

"You have to calm down," Torborg said.

"No, Jeff," I said. "This is getting personal. This stuff has to stop. Somebody is going to have to tell that little SOB, whoever he is, to bring his ass out here and face me man-to-man, and we'll end this stuff. If you don't like me or my family here, then get me out of here."

By now I was yelling at the top of my voice. The writers heard it, but none of them wrote it.

A little while later, Martin hired Willie Horton to be his "harmony" coach, and Billy approached me one day and said, "Why don't you talk trash now?"

Willie Horton was standing right behind Billy, but Willie didn't have the slightest idea what was going on.

"Let me tell you something, Billy. I come from the same side of the street as he does," I said, pointing at Willie.

I was well aware of Martin's reputation for sucker-punching guys, but I wasn't afraid and I wasn't going to back down.

"If I wanted to get after your ass, he's not going to stop me," I said.

Willie just shrugged and walked away still not knowing what it was all about, I'm sure.

I never had another problem with Billy. Of course, he wasn't around much longer, and I was gone by the time he came back for a fifth term as manager in 1988. But Junior never forgot Billy's slight, and he held the grudge all through his career. I believe that when Junior was eligible for free agency, he was quoted as saying the one team he wouldn't play for was the Yankees. Even though Martin was long gone by the time Junior reached the major leagues, some of Junior's best games came against the Yankees, and I believe psychologically that was his way of getting back at Billy Martin for dissing him when he was a kid.

The one thing that stood out that 1983 season was the Pine Tar Game on July 24. In the ninth inning, George Brett hit a two-run home run off Goose Gossage that brought the Kansas City Royals from behind and gave them a 5–4 lead over us. But Billy Martin protested that Brett hit the homer with a bat that had pine tar slathered up higher on the barrel than the rules allowed, making the bat illegal and the home run void. Brett's use of the pine tar had been noticed earlier in the season by Graig Nettles. When he told Martin about it at the time, Billy decided to keep the information to himself until such time that it would help him win a ballgame. July 24, 1983, in the ninth inning, was that time.

The umpires upheld Martin's protest, disallowed the home run, called Brett out (he went ballistic), and proclaimed us winners by the 4–3 score that preceded Brett's "home run." The Royals protested the umpires' ruling, and American League president Lee MacPhail decreed that while the umpires were accurate in following the letter of the rule, MacPhail cited the spirit of the rule and concluded that Brett's intent was not to get an unfair advantage. Therefore, MacPhail said, he was overruling the umpires, reinstating the home run, and ordering the game replayed from the point it was stopped, after Brett's home run. Billy Martin was right and Lee MacPhail was wrong. Brett used an illegal bat, and his home run should not have counted.

I didn't play in the Pine Tar Game, but when the game was resumed on August 18, I played first base in a makeshift defensive alignment that had pitcher Ron Guidry playing center field and left-handed-throwing Don Mattingly at second base.

ZOOLOGY

*"Okay, so he fined me. So what?
I was deciding whether I wanted
to be a Yankee or not."*

DESPITE IMPROVING THE TEAM DRAMATICALLY IN 1983, Billy Martin was not brought back to manage in 1984. Instead Steinbrenner replaced him with longtime Yankees favorite Yogi Berra, whose last managerial gig was nine years earlier with the New York Mets.

Toward the end of the 1983 season, the Yankees had traded center fielder Jerry Mumphrey to the Houston Astros for Omar Moreno, who was penciled in to be our center fielder. Omar couldn't hit left-handers, and Yogi knew it. One day in spring training Yogi walked over to me and said, "Hey, kid, your job is hard."

"What do you mean?" I asked.

"You have to platoon," he said.

"I have to platoon? What do you mean?" I asked.

He told me, "You have to hit against all the left-handed pitchers, and Moreno will hit against right-handers."

"You gotta be kidding," I answered.

"Uh-uh, Moreno can't hit no left-handed pitchers. You gotta hit against the left-handers. You're the only outfielder I have who can play center field and can hit left-handers," Berra said.

I realized he was right. Yogi usually was. When it came to his baseball judgment, Yogi was a lot smarter than people think he was. So when we went to Boston, I faced John Tudor and Bruce Hurst. In Baltimore, I faced Scott McGregor and Mike Flanagan, and if it was late in the game and we needed a pinch-hitter, I'd face Tippy Martinez. I faced Bud Black in Kansas City, Mark Langston in Seattle, Frank Viola in Minnesota, Geoff Zahn in California, Frank Tanana in Texas, and Willie Hernandez in Detroit. I faced every

149

left-hander in the American League. And Yogi said, "You did good against the left-handers, but you can't hit the right-handers."

Maybe that's why my average slipped 33 points to .273 and my home runs dropped from 11 to seven, but I did raise my RBI total from 46 to 56. We won 87 games, only four fewer than we had won the year before under Billy Martin, and like we had the previous year, we finished in third place. But we were 17 games behind the runaway Detroit Tigers, who went wire-to-wire to win the American League East.

Late in the season, teammates Don Mattingly and Dave Winfield were locked in a close race for the American League batting championship. A week before the end of the season they were neck and neck, and we were to finish up with four games against the Detroit Tigers, managed by Sparky Anderson.

Starting the first game of the four-game series with the Tigers, Mattingly was batting .34184, Winfield .34177. On Thursday, September 27, Mattingly had one hit in three official at-bats and was batting .34179. Winfield was 0-for-1 (he walked twice, once intentionally, and hit a sacrifice fly), and his average was at .34116.

The next day, Mattingly was 1-for-4 and his average dropped to .34118. Winfield hit a pair of doubles in five at-bats and pushed ahead of Mattingly with an average of .34168.

Mattingly went hitless in the third game while Winfield was 1-for-4, so going into the final game of the season, Winfield was in the lead at .34103 to Mattingly's .33946.

To start the final game of the season for the Tigers, with the American League batting title at stake, Sparky chose a rookie pitcher, Randy O'Neal, who not only was making his third major league start, he was a right-hander, which gave Mattingly, a left-handed hitter, an advantage over Winfield, a right-handed hitter.

In the first inning, Mattingly came up with two runners on and nobody out. The first pitch was in the dirt. Sparky called time and went to the mound to talk to O'Neal. (I played with Randy in Atlanta in 1987, and one day I asked him if he remembered what Sparky had said to him when he went to the mound that day in New York. Randy said, "He said, 'Listen, I want you to throw strikes to Mattingly.'") O'Neal's next pitch was a fastball down the middle, and Mattingly hit it for a single to load the bases. Winfield followed by grounding out to third.

In the third inning, Mattingly hit a double. Batting behind him, Winfield drew a walk on four pitches. At that point, Mattingly edged slightly ahead of Winfield by .00007. It obviously was still anybody's race, but Mattingly doubled in the fourth, flied out in the fifth, and singled in the eighth while Winnie singled in the fourth but flied out in the sixth and grounded into a force-out in the eighth.

Mattingly won the batting title with an average of .34328. Winfield's final average was .34039.

I don't want to take anything away from Don Mattingly, who was a good teammate and a great hitter. He earned the title by getting four hits under extreme pressure in the final game of the season.

At the same time, I don't want to cast any aspersions on Sparky Anderson. I don't believe his comment to O'Neal meant that he was favoring Mattingly over Winfield in the batting race. I believe he just didn't want to take the bat out of the hands of either one by walking him and to give both hitters a chance to win the title fair and square.

More craziness in Yankeeland followed in 1985. Berra began his second season as manager under Steinbrenner, who promised that Yogi would be on the job for the entire season "no matter what."

Oh, really?

Berra lasted 16 games, two short of Bob Lemon's record, and he was replaced by—are you ready for this?—none other than Billy Martin...in his fourth go on the job.

My 1985 numbers were just about what they had always been. I batted .274, hit 10 homers, drove in 69 runs, and stole seven bases.

With Billy Martin as manager, the '85 season for the Yankees was pretty much what you might expect. We improved from 87 wins in 1984 to 97 in 1985 (Martin was 91–54 after taking over from Berra) and finished two games behind the first-place Blue Jays, a marked improvement over the previous year's 17-game deficit to the Tigers.

Also typical was Billy self-destructing by making some strange and unorthodox moves and throwing a few unwarranted punches.

One night in Detroit, Graig Nettles hit one of his rare triples. He drove a ball into the triangle in center field at Tiger Stadium. Nettles chugged into third base and I came to bat. Billy had told third-base coach Don Zimmer that if he leaned against the post in the dugout, that was his sign for the squeeze play. With Nettles on third, Billy leaned against the post and Zim gave me the sign for the squeeze play. It was early in the game, and I thought it was a strange time for the squeeze, but if that's what Billy wanted, that's what he was going to get. Who was I to question Billy Martin's strategy? He was very good at generating runs.

I bunted the first pitch and fouled it off. I bunted the next pitch. Another foul. I ended up grounding out, and Zim started yelling at me and Billy was yelling at Zim, "What are you doing giving the squeeze sign?"

"You were leaning on the post," Zim said. "You told me if you leaned on the post it's the squeeze."

"Oh," Billy said, "I forgot."

Talk about strange and unorthodox moves, the most bizarre may have come in 1985, in the middle of a hot pennant race, when Martin ordered Mike Pagliarulo, a left-handed hitter, to bat right-handed against a left-handed pitcher. Pags had never hit right-handed in a game in his life, but Billy had seen him hit right-handed in batting practice and thought he had a nice swing. That gave Martin a brainstorm...or a brain cramp.

We were chasing the Toronto Blue Jays in mid-September when we went into a tailspin. We beat the Blue Jays in the first game of a four-game series at Yankee Stadium to cut their lead to a game and a half in the American League East. But then we lost the next three games and then lost a makeup game to the Indians. We flew to Detroit and lost the first game of a three-game series to the Tigers. We had fallen five games behind Toronto, and time was running out.

In the second game in Detroit, on September 18, we went into the sixth inning tied 2–2. We had runners on second and third, two outs, and Pagliarulo coming to bat against left-hander Mickey Mahler. Pags had looked futile in his first two at-bats against Mahler, striking out both times. That gave Martin an idea. He instructed Lou Piniella, his hitting coach, to tell Pagliarulo to bat right-handed. Pags thought Piniella was joking, just trying to ease the tension. Sure, Pagliarulo had taken some swings right-handed in batting practice, but not enough for him to be able to do it in a regular game, and not against pitchers who were trying to get him out.

When he realized Piniella was serious, Pagliarulo took his stance in the right-handed batter's box. I was thinking, *This could only happen in New York.* Not surprisingly, he struck out without taking the bat off his shoulder. After the game, when he was questioned by the writers who wondered why he didn't use one of the several right-handed hitters on his bench to bat for Pagliarulo, Martin's explanation was that he didn't want to take Pags' glove out of a tie game.

We wound up losing that game 5–2 and the next game 10–3 and moved on to Baltimore in a state of chaos.

We finally ended our losing streak at eight games by beating the Orioles 5–2. Even though we all realized it was probably too late to catch the Blue Jays, the victory and the end of the losing streak was cause for a celebration. Our victory came on a Saturday, in a day game, which meant there was a lot more time to celebrate than usual. And you know how professional athletes generally celebrate.

I wasn't a witness to this "celebration," but I knew several people who were, and this was their blow-by-blow eyewitness report. Billy and Ed Whitson had been at odds most of the season, disagreeing on pitch selection, lineups, the weather, the state of the union, music, just about anything. It probably figured that since they were "celebrating" in the same location, an oasis at the Cross Keys Inn in Baltimore, there would be some unpleasantness. Words were spoken, and then the speaking stopped and the two leading characters were conversing in sign language…with their hands clenched.

My sources told me that at one point, Dale Berra, who had been "celebrating" with Martin, grabbed Whitson to keep him from getting in Martin's face, and when Dale grabbed Whitson from behind to hold him, Billy sucker-punched him. In retaliation Whitson abandoned sign language and switched from conversing with his hands to conversing with his feet. He kicked Martin in the groin, causing Billy to fall over, and when he fell over, he broke his wrist.

The next day Martin was seen with a cast on his wrist. When people asked him what had happened, Billy said he broke his wrist bowling.

Apparently George Steinbrenner didn't buy Martin's bowling story. He fired him for the fourth time.

We started the 1986 season with my sixth manager in my five years in New York, Lou Piniella, a rookie manager. Piniella was my teammate with the Yankees from 1982 to 1984, and I loved playing with him. Lou was aggressive, one of the better clutch hitters in the game. Especially with a man on second when the team needed a single, he'd go in there and come through.

On the first day of spring training, Piniella called me into his office and said, "You don't have a job."

"I don't?" I asked.

"No, I want to put Danny Pasqua in the outfield. He's going to be my left fielder," he replied.

The Yankees wanted Pasqua to play. They thought they had a future star in him. He was considered one of their crown jewels. He had been a third-round draft pick a few years earlier. He was only 24 years old, he was a New York kid, and he had tremendous power. I saw Danny Pasqua hit balls farther than anybody.

"Okay, that's fine," I said. "But Lou, do me a favor. Let him play."

"What do you mean?" he asked.

I said, "I know Steinbrenner as well as you do. I've been here four years. If that kid makes a mistake, George is going to make you put a veteran out there in the outfield. If you want him to be your left fielder, let him play if he makes a mistake. I'll sit on the bench, and you won't hear a word out of me. I won't complain. You can use me as a pinch-hitter; you can do whatever you want to do with me. The only way this is going to work is if you live with his mistakes and let him play, no matter what Steinbrenner says."

"I'm the manager," Piniella said. "Nobody's going to tell me what to do."

"Okay, then let him play," I said.

"He's going to play. He's my left fielder," Piniella shot back.

"Fine," I said. "I understand that, but if he makes a mistake, you can put me in the outfield for one game, but then put him back out there. That will make you look like you know what you're doing."

But that's not what happened. Danny had a terrible spring. Maybe he was pressing, but he just didn't hit, and so they sent him down to Columbus, and guess who opened the season in left field?

Pasqua started hitting in Columbus, and the Yankees brought him back at the end of May, which made me expendable.

By 1986, the last year of my contract, New York (at least all the turmoil and foolishness of the Yankees) had begun to wear on me. There was enough turmoil in my own life. I was going through some changes. I was having marital problems because I was always away, and my family was back in Cincinnati, which did not have a team in the American League, so there were no scheduled trips there for me.

Everything just seemed to be crashing down on me, and one day I said to myself that I wasn't even going to go to the game; I was just going to stay home and think things over and see what happened.

I just skipped the game. I was sitting in my apartment in New Jersey watching *Godzilla*, so engrossed that I didn't hear the state police knocking on my door. In about the seventh inning, I decided to drive to Yankee Stadium, and when I left the apartment I heard someone say "Griffey." It was a state policeman.

"Yeah, what do you want?" I asked.

He said, "Hold it."

"I ain't no damn criminal," I said. I kept walking, got in my car, and decided, *I'm not going to no Yankee Stadium*, so I drove to the New Jersey Turnpike and headed south. I drove all the way down to Exit 6, the exit for the Pennsylvania Turnpike, and then I decided to go back. I went back to my apartment and missed the whole game.

The next day at the ballpark, someone asked, "Where were you?"

"I was at my apartment," I replied.

"You know George fined you."

"Okay, so he fined me. So what? I was deciding whether I wanted to be a Yankee or not," I said. Two weeks later I was traded to the Atlanta Braves. The Yankees got Claudell Washington, an outfielder, and Paul Zuvella, an infielder, who later told me, "I hate you, Griffey."

"Why?" I asked.

"Because you got me traded to the Yankees," came his reply.

In return the Braves got Andre Robertson—a kid from Texas the Yankees had thought was going to be their shortstop of the future—and me. Three years earlier, midway through the 1983 season, Robertson had been driving on the West Side Highway in New York late one night with his girlfriend, a Texas Longhorns cheerleader. Robertson missed a curve and crashed into a concrete median. The car flipped over, and Robertson suffered a broken neck. His passenger became a paraplegic. Robertson never regained his former prowess on the field.

That season of the accident, Robertson had taken over as the Yankees shortstop and impressed with his dazzling defense. He had unlimited promise. In 98 games that season, he batted .248. And he was only 25. He played only 102 games for the Yankees over the next two seasons before the trade to the Braves. But he never played another big-league game. Who knows, if Robertson had lived up to his potential and had the productive, lengthy career that was predicted for him, or if he had never taken that drive on the West Side Highway, the Yankees may never have drafted Derek Jeter.

The trade between the Yankees and Braves was made in the middle of June, but it wasn't announced until two weeks later. I was traded on a Sunday, and I was supposed to report to Atlanta the following Sunday, but we were in a pennant race and in the middle of 10 straight games against Boston and Toronto. Steinbrenner knew I hit well against both of those teams, so he wanted me to play against them, which I did. I hit in nine straight games for the Yankees and was 18-for-40, a .450 average, and the manager, Lou Piniella, didn't even know that I had been traded.

I got my emancipation on June 30, 1986. And even though I was going from a second-place team that ended up winning 90 games and remaining in the race until the final week of the season to a team that lost 89 games and finished in last place, 23½ games out of first, I was ecstatic about having escaped the loony bin that was the Bronx Zoo.

11

JUNIOR

There was this kid, only 17 years old,
and he was hitting one after
another out of the park.

I was greeted at home plate by Junior and Harold Reynolds after I hit that two-run homer on September 14, 1990. History was made when Junior stepped to the plate and followed my home run with one of his own—the first ever father/son back-to-back homers.
(AP Images)

It really was a special thing, being able to share a dugout and field with my son. We'll always be the first to ever achieve that. (AP Images)

I was honored to be inducted into the Reds Hall of Fame in 2004. (AP Images)

My grandson Trey and I were able to be at Busch Stadium to celebrate Junior's 500th home run with him on June 20, 2004. (AP Images)

Two great baseball families at the World Baseball Classic in 2006. From left to right, Barry Bonds, my grandson Trey, Bobby Bonds, me, and Junior. (AP Images)

Junior checks with his first-base coach (me) during a game against Japan at the 2006 World Baseball Classic. (Getty Images)

Since 2011 I've managed the Bakersfield Blaze in the Class A California League.
(AP Images)

Here I am walking out onto the field in Cincinnati on September 6, 2013, when the Reds honored the 1975 and '76 World Series–championship teams. (AP Images)

FOR ALL THE MADNESS I WITNESSED THERE, MY FOUR AND
a half seasons with the Yankees gave me the opportunity to spend
some time with my father and to get to know him. I was also able to
spend time with my son, Ken Jr., and to discover for the first time
what an awesome baseball talent he was.

When I was a Yankee and living in the New York area, my wife
and kids remained back in Cincinnati because we thought it was best
for Junior and Craig not to have to change schools. Junior was also
playing baseball summers with a travel team and progressing so well
that I didn't want to disrupt that. But he was approaching the turbulent
teenage years, and he occasionally would get into some typical young
person's mischief. He started coming to New York because he got into
a little problem at home. He was about 13 and, like a lot of kids that
age, was beginning to get antsy about driving a car. One day he was
caught trying to back his grandma's car out to take it for a spin. How
many kids have done something like that? Well, his mom caught him,
and she said, "I'm sending you to your dad."

So Junior came to New York. He got off the plane, and when he
saw me waiting for him, he began to cry. Oh, this was the end of the
world. The whole river unloaded on me. He thought I was going to
beat his little butt. Instead, I sat him down right there in the airport
and we talked. I went through this whole spiel with him.

I said, "Hey, you know right from wrong. What you did could
have gotten you into big trouble. If you wrecked the car and
somebody got hurt, then we'd have a real serious issue. You were
lucky your mom and grandma stopped you before anything like that
happened. That's fine. But you know right from wrong. So you tell
me, were you right doing what you did?"

"No."

"Okay. Now what do you want to do?"

"I don't know."

"Let's go to Yankee Stadium, and we'll take batting practice. Do you want to take batting practice?"

And that's what we did. We went to Yankee Stadium and went right to the batting cages, and I worked with him in the cages.

If I had a night game, Junior would come with me to Yankee Stadium, where he might hang out with some other kids until game time, and then I would get him a ticket and one of the kids who worked in the clubhouse would take him to his seat. To get his ticket, he'd have to come in the clubhouse. Billy Martin didn't like kids being in the clubhouse, and he would run them out. Junior never forgot that.

It soon became a regular thing on night games. I'd ask Junior, "Hey, you want to go hit?" He always said yes, and I'd take him to Yankee Stadium, very early before any of the players arrived, and he'd hit. Because the Yankees didn't want me to take him out on the field, we'd work in the batting cages under the stadium on the clubhouse level. It was just the two of us. I'd throw, and he'd hit. I told him, "This is where you're going to learn something."

Like me, Junior batted left-handed. At first he tried to emulate me. He tried to hit like I did, bent over in a crouch. I told him, "You're going to be a little taller, maybe a lot taller, than I am; you're going to have a lot more power than I have. When I was your age, I didn't have anyone to teach me how to hit. I had to learn how to hit by myself. You have me. I'm teaching you how to hit. And I'm teaching you the mental part of it, where you can understand what you can do and what you can't do. This is what's going to happen as you get better and better and better. You're going to have your own style. You're going to do your own things. And you're going to be able to do whatever you need to do if you're playing the game."

I knew he was going to be taller than me. I knew he was going to be a lot stronger than me. His physical attributes were so much better than mine. I had to polish everything I had to do, because I didn't have instruction. He had me.

I must have thrown hundreds, maybe thousands, of pitches to him in those days. How many young kids who are left-handed hitters get to hit against left-handed pitching day after day after day? That's what I did with Junior, and that's why he never had a problem hitting left-handers.

When he was about 13 I asked him what he wanted to be when he grew up. He said, "I want to be a major league ballplayer."

I said, "Oh, you do? Well this is how we're going to work it. I'm going to throw batting practice, but I'm not going to tell you what's coming. It's going to be game conditions. I'm going to be trying to get you out, and you're going to have to learn to make the adjustments. I will tell you how to make the adjustments, but you're going to have to do it."

I was only 19 years old when Junior was born, so when he was a teenager I was still playing. I was in great shape and was fortunate to be young enough to be able to throw almost as hard as the guys he was going to face if he got to the major leagues.

I threw him sliders and curveballs and change-ups, everything but the kitchen sink that I could possibly throw him from the left side. I would stand about halfway between home and the pitcher's mound and throw him fastballs as hard as I could so that the velocity would be anywhere from the high 80s to 95 miles an hour. The first couple of times I did that he cried. He literally cried because I beat him up. But he didn't quit. He stayed with it, and by the time he reached 14 years old and I was doing the same thing, I could not strike him out.

As I worked with him and was watching him every day, I could see the improvement. I was watching him closely because I was throwing him batting practice every day, and I could see how well he made adjustments. I'd throw him a slider down and away, and he'd go down and rip it to left field. We did a lot of work in those days, and Junior came to love it. He was so proud of taking batting practice at Yankee Stadium. Yankee Stadium? Are you kidding? He'd go back home to Cincinnati and tell his buddies he was taking batting practice with his dad at Yankee Stadium.

At the same time as I was throwing batting practice and helping him improve as a hitter, I was also working on the mental part of the game. I preached to him that if he ever flinched against a left-handed pitcher, then that pitcher had him. He was dead meat. I don't think Junior ever flinched, and I'm convinced one reason he became a very good hitter against lefties was that hitting off me all that time helped make him comfortable hitting against left-handers. If you have been hitting against left-handed pitching since you were a kid, you're not going to be intimidated by them, scared of them, or surprised by them when you face them as a professional.

I could tell by his swing and how the ball jumped off his bat at the age of 12, 13, and 14 that he had rare talent as a hitter. I'd watch the trajectory of the ball coming off his bat in the cage, and I could tell it would have had the distance to reach the right-field seats in Yankee Stadium. So I knew early what kind of power he had.

When he was in high school at Moeller High in Cincinnati, he hit a couple of balls into the red seats in Riverfront Stadium in high school games, but I wasn't there to see them. For some crazy reason whenever I was able to see him play, he never got a hit. He must have gone from age 12 to age 18 without getting a hit in front of me. It got so bad that his coaches would send messages to his mom that she should tell me not to come to his game. They'd send me binoculars, a not-so-subtle hint that if I insisted on going to Junior's game I should stand far away so he couldn't see that I was there and watch him hit through the binoculars.

By Junior's senior year in high school, I was with the Atlanta Braves, and we happened to be in Cincinnati for a series against the

Reds when Moeller was playing in a high school playoff game, so I went to the game. It was just a few days before the amateur draft, and the place was overrun with major league scouts and front-office executives, among them Bobby Cox, who at the time had left the field to serve as the Braves' general manager.

I looked at all these baseball people, most of whom I knew, and I said, "Who did you guys come to see?"

"Who do you think?" Cox said with a smile.

"Well, he can't hit," I said.

"Oh, yeah," Cox said.

"Okay," I said. "You tell me."

I stayed for a few innings and watched Junior bat twice. He struck out both times.

"Now I have to go to work," I said, and I took off for Riverfront Stadium.

That night I asked Junior how he did.

"I did okay," he said.

"What's okay?"

"Three-for-five with two home runs," he said.

A week later the Seattle Mariners made him the No. 1 draft pick in the country.

At the time, I was with the Braves. After Junior signed his contract, he came down to Atlanta and worked out with the Braves. Willie Stargell was Chuck Tanner's batting instructor, and he asked me, "Hey, Griff, can I work him out? I want to see what he can do."

"Yeah," I said. "Take him."

Willie took Junior to center field and showed him things that even I was never taught, like how to get rid of the ball quickly, what steps to take to field a ball and be in throwing position—all stuff Stargell had learned from Roberto Clemente, and Willie said Junior picked it up so quick.

When it was time to take batting practice, I told Junior to hit in my spot. He stepped into the cage wearing my uniform, and everybody was saying, "Damn, look at Ken Griffey hitting the ball."

Junior was 17, and he was hitting balls long out of the stadium. True, it was Atlanta Fulton County Stadium, which was set in the mountains of Georgia almost a mile high, and the ball flew out of there so easily it was called a launching pad. I expected him to hit balls out of there. It was easy for him. But I wasn't hitting the ball that far, and there was this kid, only 17 years old, and he was hitting one after another out of the park. He hadn't even grown to his full height. He was about six feet tall, a shade taller than me, and he still had another growth spurt coming. He added about three more inches in the next few years.

Junior left Atlanta and flew to Seattle, where he worked out with the Mariners before continuing on to Bellingham to launch his professional career in the Class A Northwest League. The manager of the Mariners at the time was Dick Williams. He watched Junior work out, and he told Woody Woodward, the general manager, "I'll take him on the team right now. I don't see a thing wrong with him. We don't have a player who can hit, field, run, and throw like this kid."

Nevertheless, the Mariners sent Junior to Bellingham. In 54 games, still a few months from his 18th birthday, Junior batted .313, hit 14 home runs, and drove in 40 runs.

When he started playing professionally, I tried to stay in touch with him by telephone because I was still playing myself and there was no way I could get to see him play. Even when he reached Seattle in 1989, I rarely got to see him play. You weren't getting a lot of Mariners games on national TV back then. There might be a game here and there, but because I was playing, it was rare that I could catch one of his games on TV.

If I did get to see him live and I saw something he did wrong, I'd try reaching him in the Mariners clubhouse. If Junior wasn't available, I'd talk to one of the Mariners clubhouse men and tell them to tell Junior what I saw. And Junior had the good sense to make the correction in his next at-bat.

If I saw an at-bat on ESPN and he struck out or something, I'd call him after the game or the next day, we'd talk, I'd make a suggestion, and he would make the adjustment in his next game.

I know it's often difficult for a kid if his father has had some success as a major league player. There are always going to be comparisons made. Kids are always going to want to impress their dads. I watched one kid go through that sort of thing throughout his whole life, and he couldn't live up to his father; that was Pete Rose Jr.

Since Junior was a little kid I tried to impress on him that he wasn't under any pressure to outdo me. I taught him that he has never had to impress me about anything. I told him, "You are my son first, a ballplayer second. And don't ever think that you have to impress me about anything." I told him that all he needed to do was play as hard as he could and not worry about what I did. He was never under any pressure to do better than me. Not from me he wasn't. I knew his numbers were going to be better than mine. I knew he was going to go a lot farther than I went because of his ability and his talent and how big and strong he was going to get compared to me. Not only that, he had somebody that was there 24/7 for him. That was me.

When Junior got to the big leagues in 1989, it was all rather overwhelming for him. He was so young, only 19 years old, and he was being treated like a superstar. He didn't know how to deal with all the attention. In Seattle he was looked upon as a savior, the future face of the franchise.

In his rookie year, he complained to me that he couldn't go out to dinner, to a movie, or even to a mall or a department store in Seattle because he would be hounded. There were times he had to leave a restaurant because the people bothered him so much he couldn't eat. People were intrusive. They would mob him when he went to dinner. He said, "Dad, I can't even go get something to eat. I can't go to a hamburger joint. I can't do anything." He didn't even want to go out. You're talking about a kid 19 years old. That was a tough thing for him to deal with.

I tried helping him cope with it, but I really wasn't able to relate to what he was experiencing. I was 23 when I reached the majors, and I never was the superstar that he was.

Things changed the next year when I got to the Mariners and got to play with Junior. I would suggest that he and I go out to dinner, and he'd say, "I don't know. We'll be bothered."

"No we won't," I'd say.

We'd go to dinner, maybe just the two of us, maybe with his girlfriend and whoever. People would come over looking for his autograph or asking him to pose for a picture, and I would shoo them all away.

I'd say, "He's eating. He doesn't want to be bothered. We're going to sit here and enjoy family time." I would tell everybody no, he's not signing autographs, he's not taking pictures, we're going to have a nice dinner and we're going to talk between the two of us or whoever was with us.

"You don't have to be the villain," I told him. "I'll handle it. Let me be the villain."

I just thought it was my obligation as a father first, a teammate second.

12
TIMING

They were good kids, and they played hard when they got on the field. I made it my job to help them as much as possible. If they needed to talk to somebody, they could talk to me and know that's as far as it would go.

TIMING IS EVERYTHING IN LIFE...AND IN BASEBALL. TWICE IN my career, once at the beginning and the second time near the end, my timing was impeccable. Every other time in between, my timing was horrible.

I was fortunate to arrive in Cincinnati when the Big Red Machine was at its peak, just in time to play on three National League pennant winners and two World Series champions and to play alongside three future Hall of Famers—Johnny Bench, Joe Morgan, and Tony Perez—and a fourth who should be in the Hall of Fame, Pete Rose.

After that experience, my luck ran out and my timing was terrible. I became a Yankee the year after they played in their fourth World Series in six years. They did not play in another for 14 years.

I was traded to the Atlanta Braves just as Tom Glavine and John Smoltz were coming along.

I returned to Cincinnati and left there about six weeks before the Reds won their first World Series in 14 years.

As they say, if I didn't have bad luck, I'd have no luck at all.

I'm not complaining. Not many get to play 19 seasons in the major leagues, and even fewer get to play on the same major league team as their son. And nobody, I mean *nobody,* in the history of Major League Baseball—at least not yet—has enjoyed the thrill that I experienced on the night of September 14, 1990, which I will talk about in greater detail later.

As I have already described it, my Yankees years were a jumble of confusion, turmoil, dysfunction, and frequent upheaval and change.

My two-plus seasons in Atlanta were much more serene and much less challenging. Make what you will of this, but the change from the madness in New York to the calm in Atlanta, from the American

League to the National League and from a pennant contender to an also-ran, made hardly any difference to me statistically. In 59 games with the Yankees that season, I batted .303, hit nine home runs, and knocked in 26 runs. In 80 games with the Braves, I batted .308, hit 12 homers, and knocked in 32 runs. And there was one magical night I enjoyed just 22 days after I was traded from the Yankees to the Braves: July 22, 1986. Oh, what a night!

I was not a home-run hitter, never was, and I don't tell myself that I was. My statistics say what I was. I played 19 major league seasons, 2,097 games, and had 7,229 official at-bats. I had 2,143 hits, 1,550 of them singles. I hit 152 career home runs, eight home runs per season, or one home run for every 13.5 games and one for every 47.6 at-bats. But there was one day….my 15 minutes of fame!

It came in Atlanta against the Phillies. Kevin Gross was the pitcher. I started in left field and batted third. The Phillies scored three runs in the top of the first. I came up in the bottom of the first with two outs and nobody on base, and I took Gross deep to center field.

It was 4–1 when I led off the bottom of the seventh and hit my second home run off Gross, that time to right field, to make it 4–2.

It was still 4–2 when I came to bat to lead off the bottom of the ninth and I got Gross again, another solo shot, to make it 4–3. It knocked Gross out of the game. We tied the score on a fielder's choice later in the ninth, but we lost the game 5–4 in 11 innings. Gross allowed just seven hits, and three of them were my home runs, but he had the good sense to make them all come with the bases empty.

Later one of the writers told me that on May 25, 1935, Babe Ruth, playing for the Boston Braves against the Pirates in Pittsburgh, hit three home runs in a game, the last three home runs of his 714. Five days later, he announced his retirement. He was 40 years old.

I'm no Babe Ruth, and I was only 36 when I hit my three against the Phillies. I played five more seasons and hit 39 more home runs, and there is only one of those 39 that I remember. It's one I will never forget.

To put it bluntly, we—the Braves—were not a very good team. In the parts of three years I was there, we finished sixth, fifth, and sixth and averaged 65 wins a year and did it with one bona fide star, Dale Murphy, who at the time was in the midst of six consecutive All-Star Game selections. In my three seasons in Atlanta, with very little protection in the batting order, Murphy hit 97 homers and drove in 265 runs.

In 1986, with Chuck Tanner as manager, we won 72 games and lost 89, and we regressed in the next two years. In 1987 we won 69 games under Tanner. When we got off to a 12–27 start in 1988, Tanner was replaced by Russ Nixon (Bobby Cox, who had left as manager of the Toronto Blue Jays to become general manager of the Braves, would not return to the field for two more years). Although they had three probable Hall of Famers on their pitching staff in 1988—Tom Glavine was 7–17, John Smoltz was 2–7 (Greg Maddux won 18 games, but he did that for the Chicago Cubs), and Bruce Sutter saved 14 games—the Braves won only 54 games. But I was not there to see most of it.

By the middle of the 1988 season, it was clear to me that my days in Atlanta were numbered. The Braves were in a rebuilding mode, and I knew it would be only a matter of time before they would move me out and replace me with a much younger man (23-year-old David Justice and 24-year-old Ron Gant were on the fast track from the minor leagues to Atlanta). The Braves released me on July 28. Five days later I was going *home,* back to Cincinnati where I began.

Not only was I going home, my manager with the Reds was going to be my old Big Red Machine teammate, Pete Rose. He had been there a few years, having taken over for my old minor league manager Vern Rapp for the final 41 games of the 1984 season. Pete had been with the Montreal Expos, who traded him to the Reds so that Rose could become the manager in Cincinnati. He took over as player/manager of a team that went on to finish fifth in 1984 and moved it up to second place in 1985. Whether his greatest influence in the Reds' rise was as a player or as a manager is difficult to say; it was probably a combination of the two. Pete Rose the manager was no different than Pete Rose the player—aggressive, daring, cocky, constantly in motion, talking practically nonstop.

He guided the Reds to a second place finish again in 1986. While Reds fans were delighted with the team's improvement, Pete was not. It was not in his nature to be satisfied with second place. He decided that the job of managing was too demanding for him to continue playing and that he could be a better manager if he didn't have the added burden of producing as a player, so he quit playing in 1986 at the age of 45, even though I'm convinced he had a few more years left as a player. Again he finished in second place in 1987; three years as manager of the Reds, three second place finishes.

It was Rose who lobbied the Reds to sign me after I was released by Russ Nixon in Atlanta. He brought me back to Cincinnati because he needed somebody to talk to the younger players on the team—like Eric Davis, Barry Larkin, Chris Sabo, and Paul O'Neill—and not be a threat to them. I was 38 years old; whose job was I going to threaten? He needed somebody who wasn't going to be a threat and who knew how to talk to the younger players, because Pete didn't know how to talk to them. If Sabo said he needed to do this or do that, Pete would say to him, "Hey, listen, I got 4,000 hits. How many have you got?"

That was Pete, and a lot of the younger players resented that because they knew they weren't Pete Rose. But how do you get them to play for you? When I got released in Atlanta, it was a big plus for Rose. He jumped right in and suddenly had himself what amounted to a player/coach. I could talk to the younger players as a teammate without them fearing I was a spy for the manager.

I was more than happy to be that sort of unofficial coach for Rose. He had my unrelenting loyalty for bringing me back to Cincinnati when he did. Had Rose not stepped in at the time, I might have retired on the spot. But having gone back to the Reds, I managed to squeeze three more years out of my playing career, and for that I am forever in the debt of Pete Rose.

Almost immediately, I had a very good rapport with the young players. They quickly realized I wasn't the toughest guy to come and talk to, and I truly believe they enjoyed having me there because they knew I wasn't a threat; they knew I wasn't going back and telling Pete everything these young guys were doing, because it wasn't Pete's business. They would talk to me about what was bothering them, what problems they had. They were good kids, and they played hard when they got on the field. I made it my job to help them as much as possible. If they needed to talk to somebody, they could talk to me and know that's as far as it would go. And they all became outstanding players. They all played on a World Series championship team, and one of them (Larkin) made the Hall of Fame.

Before I joined the Reds, Rose had run afoul of baseball law when he got into an altercation with umpire Dave Pallone. In the ninth inning of a game against the New York Mets, Pallone called a Mets runner safe at first. Rose disputed the call vehemently and in confronting the umpire wound up shoving him. National League president Bart Giamatti suspended Rose 30 days, the longest suspension in baseball history meted out to a manager for an on-field incident.

Tommy Helms, one of Rose's coaches, took over the team, and when Pete returned he brought the Reds home in second place for the fourth straight year. The following year Rose's real troubles began. He was suspended again, and again Helms finished out the year as manager and we fell to fifth place with a record of 75–87.

In 1990 the Reds brought Lou Piniella in to manage, and I could sense that my career was coming to a close. Lou and I had a history from our time together with the Yankees, so I wasn't expecting to be given any preferential treatment. I had the feeling that Lou considered me a threat. Why, I don't know. Didn't I demonstrate that I was on his side when he became manager of the Yankees and I tried to help him by telling him how he should treat the young Dan Pasqua?

So in spring training with the Reds in 1990, some of the writers kept telling me I might not make the team. "What do you mean?" I asked. "Who's on the bench that can outplay me?"

There was nobody. But still I had no guarantees. Then lo and behold, Todd Benzinger, our first baseman, hurt his elbow. Piniella knew I was the only guy he had in camp who could play first because he had seen me play first for the Yankees in 1983 when Lou was a player. I played first base that whole spring training, and I hit higher than .300. I was the only backup first baseman he had who also was a backup outfielder. So Piniella couldn't get rid of me. By the middle of August, Benzinger's elbow had healed and he was back at his old first-base station. Billy Hatcher, who had come over in a trade with the Pirates, had taken over in left field, and Hal Morris was doing a good job as a left-handed-hitting backup at first base and the outfield.

Only then could Lou Piniella get rid of me.

Was it merely a coincidence that when Piniella became manager of the Yankees in 1986, I was traded that June, and when he became manager of the Reds in 1990, I was being released in August?

13

ANCIENT MARINER

It finally came to pass on August 31, 1990, father and son playing together on the same team, the Seattle Mariners against the Kansas City Royals.

IT'S NEVER A GOOD THING WHEN YOU'RE 40 YEARS OLD, you're batting in the low .200s, you haven't started a game in six weeks, you're hitless in your last 19 pinch-hit appearances, and the manager calls you into his office.

Lou Piniella had a problem. He had the Reds in first place and he was trying to hold on to the lead, but then one of his starting pitchers, Tom Browning, sprained his ankle. The sprain wasn't serious enough to put him on the disabled list, but Browning was going to miss a couple of starts, and Piniella needed to find a pitcher or two to take those starts. In order to do that, he had to make room on the roster. Somebody had to go. Guess who?

I was left with some options. I could retire, but if I chose not to, the Reds would figure out another way to move me. They hoped they could convince me to agree to accept a temporary demotion to their triple A farm team (because I was a veteran, I could not be sent to the minor leagues without my permission), where I would remain until the major league rosters expanded on September 1, and then they'd bring me back.

That, to me, was completely out of the question. I had spent five years in the minor leagues, and I wasn't about to spend even another day there. No way.

I decided that my best option was to retire, but I was afraid that if I retired I wouldn't get the money I was owed by the Reds. When I mentioned that to Bob Quinn, the assistant general manager of the Reds, he said, "Don't worry; I'll get you your money."

So I decided to retire. I figured it was time anyway, and I settled into putting my head around the idea that my playing days were over and thinking about where I would go from there. (I later learned that the

Reds players had dedicated their season to me by writing my uniform No. 30 on their shoes, which was flattering and much appreciated. P.S. They went on to win the World Series).

I was watching the *Game of the Week* one day, and they were talking about me retiring, and they said that there were rumors the Seattle Mariners were interested in teaming me up with my son.

Seattle general manager Woody Woodward—a friend and teammate with me on the Reds who later was assistant general manager with the Yankees when I was there—was quoted as saying, "Ken Griffey Sr. is on the voluntary retired list and still the Reds' property. If he chooses to come back and play, he has to settle with that ballclub. We will watch the situation closely in the next week."

That was news to me. I knew nothing about it. I hadn't heard from anybody connected with the Mariners. I didn't even know Seattle wanted me.

Then I heard Tim McCarver on the *Game of the Week* say something about how if I hadn't retired, I could have joined my son right away but since I retired I had to wait 60 days before I could sign with another team. Uh-oh! That's not what I was led to believe. When I heard what McCarver said I called my agent, Brian Goldberg, and he called Reds owner Marge Schott and Bob Quinn and tried to get them to rescind my retirement announcement so that if the Mariners wanted me I would be available to join them immediately. "We're not opening a can of worms," Marge said. "He's retired; that's it," and she hung up.

Then I got a phone call from the National League president, Bill White. "What happened?" he asked.

I filled him in, and he said, "I'll get back to you."

Bill called back and said, "You're going to Seattle."

Apparently Bill used the influence of his office to get the Reds to agree to release me, which allowed any team to sign me after a 72-hour waiver period. It also meant the Reds were obliged to pay the balance of my $85,000 salary except for about $15,000 that was Seattle's responsibility.

The way I figured it, the Mariners may have been bringing me in to be a babysitter. Well, my babysitting days were over. But I was excited about joining the Mariners and playing on the same team with my son. He had been in the major leagues almost two years and I had never seen him play except on television. He was in the American League and I was in the National League. He was on the West Coast and I was on the East Coast. If I saw him, it was usually on ESPN's *SportsCenter* when they would show the plays of the day. It seemed like they were showing one of his catches almost every night.

I tried to keep up with his career as best I could. I was able to do that by speaking with him on the telephone often. Junior and I have always been competitive. He's always wanted to outdo me, which I think is a good thing. He's done a very good job at doing just that. He's made me very proud of him, but just the same, at times I have had to pat myself on the back and kind of put him in his place.

Like in his rookie season when he made that fantastic catch in Yankee Stadium, racing to the fence in center field, a little toward left, leaping up over the fence and clutching the ball in his glove hand to rob Jesse Barfield of what would have been the 200th home run of his career. Junior said, "Dad, did you see that catch?"

It just happened I had seen it. At the time, I was scouting and had to go to New York for something, and when I realized the Mariners were in town, I went to the game with a friend. We happened to be sitting next to Jesse Barfield's wife, Marla. I didn't know her and she didn't know me, and when Junior made the catch she said, "You gotta be kidding me. How did he make that catch?"

I said, "He's got pretty good hands."

The person sitting next to her said, "You know that's his dad."

And Jesse's wife said she'd never forgive me for that play.

I said, "I didn't catch it, my son did."

And Marla said, "You better talk to your son and tell him don't catch that ball like that any more off Jesse."

Barfield had hit his 199th home run in the second inning off Randy Johnson, and he eventually got No. 200 anyway, in the seventh inning, when he hit the ball so deep into the seats Junior had no chance to rob him. Later he told Junior, "I knew you weren't going to catch that one."

So if it wasn't for Junior's catch in the fourth inning, Barfield would have had three homers in the game off the great Randy Johnson.

When Junior asked me if I saw his catch against Barfield, I reminded him that some years before I had made a similar catch in Yankee Stadium to rob Marty Barrett of the Red Sox of a home run. At the time, Dick Young, the longtime New York baseball writer, called it possibly the greatest catch in baseball history. I don't know about that, but I was happy he thought so. If you look at a video of the two catches, Junior's and mine, they're very similar. Both of us leaping high over the wall to bring the ball back onto the field with our glove hand.

"The only difference in the two catches," I told Junior, "is that you're 6'3" and I'm 5'11", and when you made your catch you were 19 years old; when I made mine I was 36."

Another time he called me all excited because he threw Roberto Kelly out at home plate with a throw from deep center field to the catcher on a fly.

"Hey, Dad," he said, "did you see that play?"

"Yeah, I saw it. Why didn't you hit the cutoff man?" I asked.

"Why should I hit the cutoff man? I can throw from center field all the way to home plate on a fly," he replied.

"No, no. That's not the point. You have to play the game right. Hit the cutoff man. Play the game right," I told him.

He listened to me, and then he said, "It was on ESPN wasn't it?"

Suddenly it looked like unless there was some hitch, I was going to go to Seattle and my son and I were going to be teammates. The closer I came to getting my official release and signing with the Mariners, the more excited I became. My feeling kept getting stronger and stronger.

Up until that time, I had never even thought about playing on the same team with Junior. I just figured I'd stay with the Reds and end the season with them and then probably retire.

The one thing that concerned me about playing on the same team with my son was that I didn't want to be a distraction to him. But I eased my mind when I talked with him and I got the strong feeling that he wanted me there more than anything.

In Seattle, the team had a press conference, and somebody asked me if I was going to room with Junior on the road.

"Hell, no, I'm not going to room with him," I said, and I meant it. Why would I want to room with a 19-year-old?

Why would he want to room with a 40-year-old?

They asked me how it was going to be playing with my son and if I would do anything differently. I told them no, that I was a professional and had been playing the game for 20 years. I wasn't going to do anything differently. I did admit that I was a little nervous for Junior, because he was all excited to be playing with his dad. I already knew how to control my emotions a little better than he did.

It finally came to pass on August 31, 1990, father and son playing together on the same team, the Seattle Mariners against the Kansas City Royals. The night before, there were 10,055 fans in the Kingdome. But on August 31 there were 27,166 fans to see Randy Johnson pitching for us against Storm Davis. I was in the No. 2 hole playing left field. Junior batted third and played his customary center field.

Johnson retired the Royals in order in the top of the first, and we came to bat in the bottom of the inning. I was hitting second and playing left field. As Harold Reynolds stepped into the batter's box, I grabbed my bat and the lead donut and took my place in the on-deck circle. Harold flied out to center field, and I walked up to the plate and began the same routine I had performed for almost 20 years. First with my spikes I scraped off a line in the front of the batter's box so that I could see where I was stepping when I swung. Then I would settle into my stance and try to get comfortable, and just as I did I heard a voice from the on-deck circle.

"Come on, Dad."

Come on, Dad? I had never heard that before in the batter's box. I almost lost it right there. I had to regroup and calm myself down. From that point on, my concentration was very high. In order for me to concentrate on playing out there with him, I had to imagine he was 12 years old again and we were playing in the backyard.

The first pitch from Storm Davis was a ball. I swung at the next pitch and lined a single to center field.

In the days that followed, I went on a tear at the plate. It may have been the change of scenery or the new lease on life I got in Seattle. And it may have been that I was pumped because I was playing with my son.

I appeared in 21 games with the Mariners and batted .377 with three home runs and 18 runs batted in. Someone told me that when Marge Schott learned what I was doing in Seattle, she exploded. "He's hitting over .300 in Seattle, and he hit only .206 here," she told one of her Reds employees. To make matters worse for Marge, she noticed that the Mariners' attendance spiked after I got there. They drew 27,166 in my first game, an increase of more than 17,000 fans from the previous game. The next game, they drew 24,160. And then 17,307 and 25,129, and then to really burn her, they drew 55,679 against the Chicago White Sox on September 21.

Marge called Woody Woodward, the Mariners general manager, and said she wanted half the gate receipts when Junior and I played together.

That time Woody hung up on *her.*

14
ROSE

The Pete Rose I know played hard, and he played to win. He hated to lose as much, or more than, anybody I have ever known.

REPORTS SURFACED EARLY IN 1989 THAT INFORMATION WAS discovered connecting Pete Rose to wagers made on some baseball games. When questioned in the matter by the outgoing baseball commissioner, Peter Ueberroth, Rose denied the allegations and the investigation was dropped. That should have been the end of it. It wasn't.

Soon after Ueberroth left office, his successor, A. Bartlett Giamatti, retained attorney John Dowd to investigate the charges against Rose. Dowd's findings, which were never made public, apparently provided such an indictment against Rose that, to avoid public disgrace, Pete had no choice but to voluntarily accept being placed on baseball's permanent ineligible list. This meant that Rose could take no part in any official function of the Cincinnati Reds or Major League Baseball. To Rose the most hurtful and controversial consequence was that he became ineligible for election to the Baseball Hall of Fame, where his playing record demands he belongs.

Consequently, the name Pete Rose has never appeared on the National Baseball Hall of Fame ballot, which lists those eligible for election to the Hall of Fame and is distributed to 10-year voting members of the Baseball Writers' Association of America.

Hardly a year goes by when debate does not arise over the pros and cons of Pete's election to the Hall, all of the dialogue in vain because the customary 15-year period of eligibility for election passed years ago.

I go back with Pete more than 40 years, and I find him to be among the most polarizing athletes ever, a combination of Muhammad Ali, Alex Rodriguez, Mike Tyson, and Michael Jordan. You can like him or you can loathe him—and to clarify my position, I stand firmly on the former side—but you can't ignore him.

Not many people know what Pete went through when he was a young player. When he broke in, in 1963, Pete was the victim of reverse racism. He came up as a second baseman, and some of the veterans resented him because he was taking the job away from one of their buddies, Don Blasingame. The only guys Pete could hang around with were the young black guys: Frank Robinson, Vada Pinson, and Tommy Harper.

As years went on, Pete hung around with Lee May and Tony Perez. Rose and Bench never got along until lately. They have finally started to talk after more than 50 years. J.B. is getting older and more mellow, and now he's a lot more fun to be around than when he was a cocky kid.

There has been a lot of talk lately about bullying in professional sports, the hazing by veteran players who demean, denigrate, and even dehumanize rookies in the name of team spirit and camaraderie. In my day, it was just the reverse. Veterans would look after rookies, mentor them, counsel them, support them, and even aid them financially. And Rose was at the top of the list in mentoring. Later, when he was established and Hal McRae came up and George Foster came up and I came up, Pete took care of the young players. I know, because I was the recipient of his caring. If a group of us were in a restaurant and Pete came in, he would pick up the check. For a while the Reds had us wear red jackets when we traveled; Pete bought red jackets for all the rookies.

I always respected Pete for that, even though I know all the things he went through. I always said Pete is going to be Pete. I say that without malice. No matter how we look at it, no matter what people think of him, he's going to be Pete Rose. He always thought he was bigger than baseball in some ways. And that wasn't the case, as everybody finds out sooner or later. Anyone who thinks that way sooner or later finds out it doesn't work that way. Baseball is going to be around a lot longer than all of us who have played the game, a lot longer even than those who played it better than anybody else and think they're bigger than baseball, or football or basketball.

My son Ken Junior and Pete's son Pete Junior practically grew up together. Little Petey is five days older than my Junior, and Petey would hang around Junior all the time because Pete couldn't do any father/son stuff. The people would mob Pete for autographs if he went out in public, so it was difficult for him to spend any quality time with his own son.

I told Pete that Little Petey could come with me. If I was taking my two sons, Junior and Craig, places, I invited Little Petey to come along so that he had some other kids to go with and do kids' stuff with. I'd take them on go-karts, or to a movie, just the thing kids do. Pete said, "Thanks, man, that really helps me out a lot."

I enjoyed playing with Pete Rose, and I especially enjoyed watching him play. I'd never tell him this, but I wanted to be like him. Everything he did, he did 150 percent. His work ethic was off the charts. During spring training he would get to the ballpark at 7:00 or 8:00 in the morning back in the days when spring training began at 10:00 AM. By that time, Pete would have spent three hours hitting in the batting cage. He had his own routine. He'd get on that Iron Mike, a pitching machine, and he'd move halfway between the mound and home plate and swing one-handed working first the left hand and then the right. He'd do that for about a half hour, and then he'd move back a few feet and do it again for another half hour. By the time he got back to home plate, he had adjusted to the speed that to him felt like he was hitting a change-up. He did that every day. He wouldn't wear batting gloves, and he worked his hands until they were red and raw, and then he poured Tuff Skin on them and he worked his hands some more. When the games started, his hands were so tough and there were blisters everywhere.

He'd take 200 to 300 ground balls every day, depending on where he was playing. They asked him to move from second to third base, left field, right field, third base. It didn't matter. He'd still take ground balls. He took ground balls until the guy hitting them got tired.

He was a great person and a statistics nut. He knew everything about every player in the league. I'd ask him, "Pete, who we facing two weeks from now?" And he'd tell me exactly what pitchers we were going to face.

Put me down as one of those who believe Pete Rose belongs in the Hall of Fame, and I'll never change my opinion on that. I believe he belongs because of what he did on the field—4,256 hits, a lifetime average of .303 for 24 seasons, 10 seasons with at least 200 hits, 10 seasons with at least 100 runs scored, 19 seasons in which he played in no less than 148 games, a guy who played hard, played hurt, played to win, sacrificed his body, busted it to first base on every ground ball he ever hit, and played past his 45th birthday and quit playing only because he felt he needed to concentrate his energy and his focus on managing. Pete Rose not in the Hall of Fame? Are you kidding me?

All the other stuff they say he did, I know it was wrong, because they had that big sign in every clubhouse that said GAMBLERS NOT ALLOWED. But I don't know if he gambled when he was a player. I have no idea. I don't think he did, but I don't know. All that stuff only came out when he was a manager.

I have known Pete Rose since the early 1970s. I played with him as a teammate and for him as a manager, and I have never heard or seen any indication that he bet on baseball. He may have bet on basketball games or football games and participated in football pools, but that would have been out of the baseball season, so I would not have been aware of it.

I know Pete liked to go to the racetrack and that he enjoyed casino gambling. Was Pete Rose the only player, coach, manager, general manager, or owner who went to the racetrack? Was he the only player, coach, manager, or general manager who bet on horses, went to casinos, bet on football, or owned horses?

Going to the racetrack or the dog track was just about the only recreation baseball guys could get during the season when they had so much leisure time on their hands. What can a ballplayer do to pass the time when his work is done in spring training, which is very long and can get boring? Maybe he doesn't play golf. Maybe he doesn't want to spend a few hours in a bar drinking. In Tampa, there was no racetrack, so Pete would go to the dog track. And he wasn't the only one.

The Pete Rose I know played hard, and he played to win. He hated to lose as much, or more than, anybody I have ever known. He was the fiercest competitor and the hardest worker I have ever known. He loved and respected the game of baseball. That's why I find it hard to believe that he bet on baseball, certainly not as a player and not even as a manager, not against his team and not even for his team to win.

As great a game as baseball is, it has problems today with players taking PEDs, performance-enhancing drugs. Cheaters! Pete Rose has never been accused of taking steroids or PEDs. He has never been accused of cheating on any one of his 15,890 major league plate appearances.

He belongs in the Hall of Fame. He's already in mine.

15

GAMESMANSHIP

I never got a bunt sign. I never saw a sign of any kind. We didn't even have a third-base coach. You had to rely on your instincts.

THE GAME OF BASEBALL SOUNDS SIMPLE ENOUGH. SO WHY has this great game undergone such widespread changes? Why have such buzzwords as *steroids*, *PEDs*, *free agency*, *designated hitter*, *wild card*, and *pitch count* been added to the game's lexicon while the words *complete game* have been all but deleted?

I am fortunate enough to have spent more than a half century earning a paycheck in the game I love, and to have done it on just about every level, from minor league player to major league player to major league coach, scout, instructor, and minor league manager. And I have learned that players on every level are all the same.

The game is still played pretty much the same way it has been played since they moved the pitcher's mound back from 45' to 60'6" back in 1893, and the players playing it—most of them at least—still play the game as hard as they ever did. Sure, there are some players who make so much money and have seven-, eight-, 10-year contracts that they think they can just go through the motions. But most of today's players have a lot of personal pride. To me that's the biggest thing about players. If you don't have personal pride in what you're doing, you're not going to play well. But if you think of yourself as a good player and you work hard and play hard, you will be rewarded.

It's unfortunate that the game has just gone through the scourge of the steroids era, in which players have been unfairly victimized. And that includes Junior. I can't speak for most players, but I think I can speak for my own son. I know he has not done anything illegal as far as using steroids or PEDs, but years from now people are going to look at his numbers, the 630 home runs, the 1,836 runs batted in. They're going to notice that he played in the steroids era, and they're going to come to an unfair conclusion.

I came up in an era when even lifting weights was considered taboo for baseball players. The prevalent thought in my day was that lifting weights made one muscle-bound, and hitters needed supple muscles in order to generate bat speed. That theory was still being preached when Junior came into pro ball in the late 1980s (it changed later when hitters began pumping iron to get stronger and then graduated to using PEDs and steroids to boost their power numbers), so he never even lifted weights. He did a lot of cardio, bicycling and stuff. He believed in that wholeheartedly. He never would lift weights.

People always said Junior was a natural hitter. That wasn't true. He worked to get where he was. People don't know how hard he worked. He would take batting practice for hours to fine-tune his swing.

The other part of Junior's success was the mental part of the game. He was so confident in his ability to do things on the baseball field, and that helped him do the improbable. He had the kind of mental discipline and physical ability that, if he said he was going to do something, he would concentrate so hard that he would do what he said he was going to do. That's how focused he was.

I was the same way, but in my case I had no choice. I looked at things totally differently than he did. I had to feed a family. He was going to feed his family. That was never an issue with Junior. With him it was a matter of pride to be the best at what he was doing.

It's unbelievable that Junior put up the numbers he did when you realize how much time he missed because of all the injuries he suffered and the mental stress he was under.

In the strike-shortened 1994 season he led the league with 40 home runs, playing in 111 of 112 games, but in 1995 he broke his wrist, playing in just 72 games with 17 home runs. That's 57 home runs in two years combined, at a time when he had been averaging 50 home runs a season. After going to Cincinnati in 2000 and playing 145 games for the Reds, he played in 111, 70, 53, 83, 125, and 109 games over the next six years, all in his prime years of 31 to 36. And still he hit 630 career home runs. I have no doubt that if he had stayed reasonably healthy throughout his career, Junior would have hit between 900 and 1,000 home runs. Without steroids!

Then there was the mental pressure. He was the face of the Mariners, but he was traded to the Reds before the 2000 season because the Mariners had Alex Rodriguez and they thought they had Junior's successor to carry them. But at the end of that season, as soon as his time was up, A-Rod said "I'm done, I'm not going to stay in Seattle," and he got out of there and signed that obscene $252 million contract with the Texas Rangers.

When Junior left Seattle, he got all kinds of death threats from Mariners fans—not only against him, but they threatened to kill his kids or to kidnap them, which really preyed on his mind, Junior being so family-oriented. If his wife was late arriving to a game, he couldn't concentrate because he was worried about her.

Many of his injuries occurred because he tried so hard for the great catch. That grew out of a little game I would play with him when he was very young. When he was 9, 10, 11, and 12 years old I'd take him out and do little drills. I'd toss a ball in the air for him to catch, but I'd purposely toss it out of his reach so that he had to run to get it. At first he couldn't reach it, and he'd complain, "I can't catch that."

"Don't say you can't. Just try and see what happens," I told him.

The next one I would toss a little closer to him, and he'd run and almost catch it. I kept tossing the ball a little closer each time, and soon he'd be thinking, *I can get that.*

"What do you think now?" I asked.

"That was easy," he replied.

"That was the same distance away from you as the one I threw before that you said you couldn't catch," I told him.

After a while, from the time he was in high school and right up to the major leagues, he believed that he could catch any ball that wasn't going out of the ballpark. There wasn't a ball hit in play that he didn't think he could catch. That's how he went about playing the outfield, and that's what caused many of the injuries. It was because he played with such reckless abandon.

I often told him, "Sometimes you have to play a ball on the first bounce to keep the double play in order."

He'd say, "Aw, Dad," which told me that he was playing to make the highlights.

The use of steroids has had a strong influence on much of the game's strategy. For a long time, managers in both leagues for the most part abandoned the running game, moving runners, employing little ball to manufacture runs, watching the lineup turn over and figuring which of the opposing hitters you were going to try to make your "out" men and which you were going to pitch around. Instead they played for the three-run homer, because players were getting so big. You look at some of those guys and how big they got from one year to the next. That doesn't happen just by lifting weights.

When you see that a guy hits two home runs one year and then hits 40 home runs the next year, you know something is wrong. It's unnatural for a hitter to improve so much so soon, but some people would do anything to get that big contract. I have to be honest, if I was in a situation where I had to support my family and needed to get a contract like some of those guys got, I'm not so sure that I wouldn't be tempted.

It was in the late 1990s, during the home-run battle between Mark McGwire and Sammy Sosa that the game changed dramatically. Home-run production was up in those years, but now that Major

League Baseball and the Players Association have cracked down on steroid use and drug testing has improved, home runs are down and some of the old strategy is coming back, and that's a good thing.

I got a pretty good primer on the care and feeding of today's young players as manager of the Bakersfield Blaze in the Class A California League, where most of my players were just starting their professional careers.

First, a little history about the Blaze and Bakersfield, which, except for the weather, was not unlike my native Donora in that its industries included natural gas, mining, and petroleum refineries, and its air pollution rate was very high.

After the 2010 season, the Reds left Lynchburg and were looking for a Class A affiliate as a replacement. At the time, the Texas Rangers had dropped their team in Bakersfield, so the Reds filled the gap and asked me to manage the team. Being the good company man I am, I agreed, and the first complication in the arrangement was that Bakersfield was as far away and as inaccessible to Cincinnati as possible. The second was the ballpark.

Sam Lynn Ballpark was built in 1941, and from the looks of things, it has never been renovated. The center-field fence is an easily reachable 354 feet, and Sam Lynn is one of only two ballparks in professional baseball that was built with home plate facing west. Consequently, in the early evening the sun shines right into home plate and into the eyes of the batter. As a result, night games that normally would start at 7:30 p.m. might start at 7:58 or later depending on what time the sun goes down.

Despite the inconveniences, the Bakersfield Blaze has a rich baseball tradition. Some of the men that sat in the same manager's office that I did were Floyd "Babe" Herman, former Phillies general manager and manager Paul Owens, Mel Queen, Kevin Kennedy, Rick Dempsey, and Graig Nettles.

Among the players who played in Bakersfield are Hall of Famer Don Drysdale, Pedro Martinez, Mike Piazza, Eric Karros, Johnny Callison, and Mike Garcia, and current stars Chris Davis, Jonny Gomes, Josh Hamilton, Joe Nathan, and James Shields.

It was in my capacity as Bakersfield's manager that I learned to come to grips with the dreaded "pitch count," something that was not a factor in my playing days. I found that to be the hardest thing for me to deal with as a manager. Kids would come to me who had never pitched a complete game. Many had never gone beyond five innings. This has only gotten worse. It starts when kids are in high school, continues in college, and then in the low minor leagues. By the time these pitchers get to the big leagues, many of them aren't even developed, because of the pitch count. When pitchers get to about 90 pitches, most of them run into a brick wall, and they can't go any farther.

I had Tony Cingrani, who was outstanding in the minor leagues and is up with the Reds. He had a pitch count of 90 to 110 pitches, and I had to abide by it. One night he had a no-hitter through six innings, and I had no choice—I was forced to take him out of the game, and the opponents weren't even close to hitting him.

I still don't know where the pitch count came from. I figure it had to come from computers, from people in the game now that are computer geeks who have never thrown a ball or put on a jock strap, yet they're making decisions about kids in the minor leagues. That's tough to take sometimes for someone who came through in an era when there were no computers and thus no pitch counts.

I understand that the reason for the pitch count is to protect the arms of the young pitchers, especially those who received big bonuses from the team. The fallacy in the thinking is that it has been proven that the arm benefits and gets stronger from use. Old-timers like to say that the arm will rust out before it wears out.

Pitchers like Nolan Ryan, who threw 100 miles an hour before radar guns were used and who pitched into his forties; Jim Kaat, who pitched until he was 44; Jesse Orosco, who pitched in 1,252 games; and Robin Roberts, who threw 305 complete games in 19 seasons never had a sore arm.

When I came through the minor leagues, the thing that our coaches stressed was fundamentals. And that's what helped me survive, because I didn't have the great Roberto Clemente arm, but I realized if I hit the cutoff man every time, that would stop the play.

I learned the fundamentals in the minor leagues from people like Russ Nixon, Jim Snyder, George Scherger, and Vern Rapp. I wasn't going to learn fundamentals in the big leagues. I played five years in the minor leagues, and that's where I had to learn in order to succeed. Now players are coming up after a year, two, maybe three in the minor leagues, and many of them are so weak in their fundamentals that they have to be taught in the major leagues, and that's hard to do. In my day, you weren't coming to the big leagues to learn. You either knew or you were sent back.

One thing that's helped is that college baseball is much better now than it was in my day. Today you have former major league players coaching in college, like Tony Gwynn at San Diego State, and now a college head coach will have a staff of four or five assistants, a pitching coach, a hitting coach, a bench coach. So much of the instruction that used to have to be done in the minor leagues now is done in college.

When I played baseball at Donora High School, the coach taught us one thing: how to go after foul balls. That was it. He hardly ever even watched the game. I never got a bunt sign. I never saw a sign of any kind. We didn't even have a third-base coach. You had to rely on your instincts. And playing in the northeast, because of the terrible weather in April and May, I probably didn't play more than 20 or 30 games in four years of high school ball. That's why people in Donora thought of me as a football player and wondered why I went to baseball instead.

I'm just glad I did.

16

BACK-TO-BACK

When the inning ended we were jogging in, and I could barely move I was hurting so bad.

I HAVE HAD MORE THAN MY SHARE OF THRILLS, HIGHLIGHTS, and success in a 19-year major league career. I have played on two World Series championship teams; made the All-Star team three times; played with Hall of Famers Johnny Bench, Joe Morgan, Dave Winfield, and Tom Seaver; and played against all-time greats Willie Mays and Henry Aaron; and I even had a surprising (for a non–home run hitter) three-homer game. Yet the No. 1 highlight in my career was to have played on the same team, in the same game, and in the same outfield as my own flesh and blood, my son Ken Griffey Jr., or Junior, as he will be referred to here.

There have been quite a few father-and-son major leaguers, but how many have played together on the same team, in the same game, and in the same outfield? The Bondses, Bobby and Barry, never did. Neither did the Fielders, Cecil and Prince; the Alous, Felipe and Moises; the Alomars, Roberto Sr., Roberto Jr., and Sandy; the Perezes, Tony and Eduardo; the Boones, Bob, Bret, and Aaron; or the Bells, Gus, Buddy, and David. Shall I go on?

The Raines, Tim Sr. and Tim Jr., actually played on the same team and in the same outfield, but that was in the final four games of the 2001 season when the Baltimore Orioles acquired Tim Sr. from the Montreal Expos for the express purpose of teaming him up with Tim Jr. Senior pinch-hit in two games and played in the outfield in two games, but it was clear that the whole thing was a gimmick, done strictly for publicity.

That wasn't the case with me. After I was released by the Cincinnati Reds near the end of the 1990 season, I signed with the Seattle Mariners and played in 21 games for them. I started 19 games in left field and batted second, behind Junior, 15 times and third four times.

The Griffey-Griffey tandem worked well enough for the Mariners to plan on duplicating it in 1991 with the elder Griffey (me) at 41 years of age batting second and playing left field. Fate had another plan.

It happened in spring training in Phoenix, Arizona. I was leaving the Mariners workout, driving on 48th Street, a four-lane highway, on my way to the doctor's office to take my customary annual preseason physical. I was going to hook up there with Harold Reynolds and Junior and a few others, but when I failed to show, they started worrying. What happened was that on my way to the doctor's office I was coming to a stoplight when I noticed a funeral procession coming across the highway from the right, so I slowed down and prepared to stop to allow the procession to pass. There was a car behind me going about 50 miles an hour, and he either didn't realize everyone had slowed down because of the funeral procession or there were cars blocking his view. I stopped, but the car behind me never stopped. He rear-ended me and knocked me almost into a McDonald's on the sidewalk to my right.

I was shaken up, but I felt okay, probably because of the adrenaline flowing in my body. A few days later, I was in pain, and I started the season on the disabled list. I was activated on April 16, the eighth game of the season.

It's hard to say who was more delighted that I was back—me because I missed the game so much or Junior because he missed needling me so much. Like the time I was camped under a fly ball in left field ready to make a catch and he came across and reached over the top of me and took it away from me. All he had to do was call me off; he didn't have to just catch it. If he had said "I've got it," I'd have moved, but he never said anything. He's a lot taller than I am, about three or four inches taller. I understood why he did it—because he's the center fielder, and the center fielder is trained to take anything he can reach, but I suspect he had the whole thing planned for some time as his way of pulling a practical joke on his father.

The ball was hit more toward left-center than straightaway-center, and he was coming pretty fast and he just snatched it. I didn't know where the ball was, because I ducked. I thought the ball dropped, and I was looking for it on the ground when I heard Junior say, "Dad, you know you got to let the sure hands have it."

It was the third out of the inning, and as we were trotting off the field, I looked up at the big screen and could see he had his glove over his mouth and was laughing all the way to the dugout. When I saw that, I was so mad at him I was ready to kill him. Later, I realized he must have planned it all along. He was being a kid, and I was being a parent. That was when the teammate in me disappeared and the parent came out. There I was standing with egg on my face, and you could hear everybody in the stadium roaring, they were laughing so hard. But I wasn't too thrilled with it.

I ran in, and I got to him and said, "Come here, I have to talk to you."

"What?" he said.

"Your little ass is grounded. Don't even talk to me. Give me the car keys; you're not driving anymore," I said.

He busted out laughing.

"Dad," he said. "You know I'm 21."

As the days went by, I began to hurt more and more. My back was hurting, my neck was hurting. I was in a lot of pain. We had a three-game series in Texas at the end of May and the beginning of June. I missed the first game of the series and started the second game on May 31. There was a ball hit to left-center field. It wasn't that far from me, but Junior ran after it from center field and threw it to third base, trying to get the runner going from first to third.

"Dad, what's wrong?" Junior asked.

"Nothing."

"Then how come you weren't running after the ball?" he asked.

"I was running as hard as I can run," I replied.

"Dad, you didn't even move."

When the inning ended we were jogging in, and I could barely move I was hurting so bad. I couldn't even lift a bat, and I couldn't turn my head to the right. If you're a left-handed hitter like me, you have to be able to turn your head to the right in order to see the pitcher. They took me out of the game and sent me back to Seattle, where they put me in traction. But that didn't help, so they sent me to Cincinnati, to Dr. William Tobler, who was one of the best neurological surgeons in the world. He discovered a bulging disc in my neck. That meant I was back on the disabled list. I underwent surgery and was finished playing baseball for the year; in fact, I was finished playing baseball for good.

The worst part about it was that I was having a pretty good year, batting .282 in 30 games. I felt I still could have played at a high level. If not for the auto accident in spring training, I think I could have enjoyed a few more years playing alongside my son.

Playing in the major leagues with my son was a joy beyond compare and something I never imagined would come about. I didn't think I'd be around that long to play with him, but I was, and I didn't think he'd get there that quick, but he did. I like to think that, in addition to the obvious, I had something to do with him being the ballplayer he was. There were all the pitches I threw to him in batting practice, but just as important were the talks we had.

I wanted to instill in him certain values that he could carry with him throughout his career. One of the things I always talked to him about was how I wanted him to make sure he enjoyed playing the game, and that's what he did. I also preached that he must respect the game and respect his opponents, and he did that. He made me a very proud dad, because he went out there and played the game hard, and he did it all the right way.

When I got to Seattle and I was watching Junior play every day up close, he opened my eyes. He was amazing. I knew he was good, but I didn't know how good he was until I played with him. I suppose before I played with him, I was focusing on his mistakes because I wanted to be his teacher; I wanted to help him correct those mistakes. But playing with him, I could see day in and day out how much talent he had—the arm, the speed, the power, the consistency.

I was the father, the veteran, a 20-year professional, but in Seattle he was the star. I was in his shadow. That didn't matter to me. I didn't need to be the star. I had my day. This was his time. I told him, "This is your team, not mine." I was just there having fun, and he was telling everybody, "I'm playing with my dad."

Playing with my son every day was a thrill. And then there was one special day...or night, Friday, September 14, 1990, in Anaheim, California. We were playing the California Angels. Kirk McCaskill, a right-hander from Ontario, Canada, and a former professional hockey player, was on the mound for the Angels. He started the game by walking Harold Reynolds on a 3–1 pitch. I was aware that Reynolds liked to steal bases (he led the league with 60 steals in 1987 and went on to steal 31 in 1990), so I tried to go deep in the count to allow Harold to steal second.

When the count went to 0–2, I was in hitting mode. McCaskill threw me a fastball—I played four and a half seasons with the Yankees, I hit in front of guys like Dave Winfield, Don Baylor, and Don Mattingly, and I didn't get as many fastballs to hit as I got in a month of hitting behind Junior. I couldn't believe all the fastballs I was getting. I got fastballs from Mike Boddicker! Mike Boddicker, who didn't have a fastball, who never threw a pitch that hit 90 miles per hour on the radar gun, who threw a whole bunch of junk, threw me fastballs when I was hitting in front of Junior. I thought, *I could make a living hitting in front of this kid. I wish I was hitting in front of this kid when I was a kid.*

So McCaskill threw me a fastball, and I got into it and drove it to center field just to the left of the batter's eye. It sailed over Devon White's head into the seats. I rounded the bases, and when I passed third base and was approaching home plate, Junior was standing there waiting for me. He was going to be the first one to greet me.

"That's the way you do it," I said.

"Way to go, Dad," he said, and when I looked into his eyes, I told myself, "His mind-set is, he's going to hit a home run; he wants to hit a home run right now."

I had hit two home runs earlier for the Mariners with Junior batting behind me. On September 7, in Boston, I hit one in the first inning against Boddicker. Junior followed me at bat and walked. On September 10 against the Oakland Athletics in Seattle, I hit a three-run homer off Bob Welch in the fourth inning. Junior followed me at bat and bounced back to the pitcher. I could tell that both times, Junior was trying to hit a home run and failed. So looking into his eyes in Anaheim, I knew he was going to try to hit a home run. I even mentioned it to Harold Reynolds.

Harold and I had touched home plate, and we walked to the end of the dugout and were standing there watching Junior hit. The count went to 3–0. Manager Jim Lefebvre gave Junior the hit sign, and he swung at the 3–0 pitch from McCaskill and sent a drive deep to center field. *Sonofagun,* I thought, *he hit it out.* The ball landed in the seats a few feet to the left of where mine landed…and a few rows deeper. I was trying my best to keep my emotions in check, knowing it was the first time in baseball history (and probably the last) that father and son hit back-to-back home runs in a major league game.

And then Junior came around the bases, a big ear-to-ear grin spread across his face as he crossed home plate and headed right to where I was standing in the dugout. When he reached me, he said, "Hey, Dad, *that's* the way you do it."

"Yes son," I said. "That *is* the way you do it."

AFTERWORD

KEN SENIOR WAS SO WELL RESPECTED BY THE MARINERS players because most of us grew up watching him play, and he was such a good player, so we were all happy to have him with us. What really made the father-son thing work was that by the time Senior arrived, Junior was already somewhat established (even though he was so young) so it wasn't a gimmick. They were two really good ballplayers.

That's my first recollection of how Senior was received. The second is that he made everybody better. Wow! Just picking his brain, talking situations with him, stuff like that was terrific. I loved it. I was sad when he hurt his back the second year and couldn't come back.

Senior and Junior didn't room together, but of course they spent a lot of time together. It was cool. They had a father/son relationship, no doubt.

The other thing that made it work was that Senior recognized that Junior was a star. If he didn't recognize that, it could have been ugly. After all, Senior was a star player himself.

I think having his father there helped Junior's transition. He was moving into that stardom stage, and he was still only 20. They did a lot of interviews together, and that allowed Junior to see how his dad handled interviews. It helped Junior grow up. His first year, before his father came aboard when Junior was only 19 and had all that fame shooting at him, he went, "Whoa, hold on here. I'm not doing that. I'm not talking. What's everybody want to talk to me for?"

I think having his father there gave him a great buffer and great example of how to handle things.

People remember the back-to-back home runs, and for good reason. It was cool, and it had never happened before that father and son hit back-to-back home runs. But I remember other things like Senior getting ready to catch a fly ball and Junior calling him off and stepping in front of him to catch the ball. That was Junior's favorite part of the game. He waited for a fly ball to come to left-center so that he could call his dad off, knowing that his dad had to let him have it because Junior was the center fielder.

I have always believed that Junior's No.1 goal in life was to be a dad like his dad. That's what he wanted to do, more than hitting all the home runs and more than going to the Hall of Fame. Junior loves his kids, and that has a lot to do with his mom, Birdie, and Senior, the way they raised him and the way Junior adored his mother and father.

—Harold Reynolds

APPENDIX

WHEN JACK DOSCHER BROKE IN WITH THE CHICAGO CUBS in 1903, he became the first son of a Major League Baseball player to follow his father's career path. It was the only noteworthy part of the younger Doscher's baseball career. In five major league seasons he appeared in 27 games with a record of 2–10.

Dad, however, did not fare much better. In 109 games from 1872 to 1882 with the Brooklyn Atlantics and Washington Nationals of the National Association, and the Troy Trojans, Chicago White Stockings, and Cleveland Blues of the National League, Herm Doscher, an outfielder/infielder, batted .225.

Since the Doschers started something, there have been slightly more than 200 offspring who have entered the family business, some with singular success, proving that the baseball, like the apple, doesn't fall far from the tree.

Here, then, chosen from several sources and presented in descending order, is the consensus choice most successful father-son combinations. (Editor's Note: Ken wouldn't add Junior and himself to the list, though we think it's apparent they would sit at the top.)

My Top Fathers and Sons in Baseball History

The Franconas: Tito the elder (son Terry honors his father by also answering to the name Tito) was born and raised in Aliquippa, PA, just a long home-run distance from my birthplace of Donora. He had a better playing career than his son and a better career than he is given credit for. A career .272 hitter with 1,395 hits, 125 home runs, and 656 runs batted in for eight teams over a 15-year, 1,719-game major league career, Francona tied with Rocky Colavito as runner-up to Hall of Famer Luis Aparicio in the 1956 American League Rookie of the Year balloting, batted a career-high .363 in 1959 (his average was 10 points higher than the AL batting champion Harvey Kuenn, but Francona failed to qualify for the title because of too few at-bats), and was a member of the 1961 American League All-Star team.

While son Terry's playing career (a .274 average, 474 hits, 16 homers, 143 RBIs for five teams in 708 games over 10 years) paled in comparison to his father's, the younger Francona earned fame as a manager with three teams, including the Boston Red Sox, whom he led to their first World Series championship since 1918. As manager of the Cleveland Indians, he was voted American League Manager of the Year in 2013.

The Sislers: Once again the father outdid the son, or in this case sons, as George Sisler was one of the game's all-time greats, a member of the Hall of Fame, a two-time American League batting champion, and a lifetime .340 hitter (tied with Lou Gehrig for 16th on the all-time list). He had 257 hits in 1920, which was a major league record that lasted for 84 years until it was broken by Ichiro Suzuki.

Sisler's three sons all had baseball careers. Dick Sisler was a .276 hitter with 55 home runs and 360 RBIs in 799 games with the Phillies, Cardinals, and Reds and had a 121–94 record as a manager in parts of three seasons with Cincinnati.

Dave Sisler had a 38–44 record as a pitcher with the Red Sox, Tigers, Senators, and Reds.

The eldest Sisler child, George Jr., had a distinguished career as a baseball executive and was the longtime president of the International League.

The Gwynns: It's burdensome enough to be the son of an all-time baseball great and even more burdensome when you have the same name as that person. Tony Gwynn Sr. was elected to the Hall of Fame as an eight-time National League batting champion, a lifetime .338 hitter (tied for 18th on the all-time list), and the producer of 3,141 hits (19th all-time). Tony Gwynn Jr. had a career batting average of .244 and 365 hits, but he did manage to play seven seasons in the major leagues.

The Bells: A family of three generations of major leaguers. Gus was the patriarch, a four-time all-star and four-time 100-RBI man with the Cincinnati Reds (he also played for the Pirates, Braves, and Mets), who batted .281 in a 15-year, 1,741-game career. He also had 1,823 hits, 206 home runs, and 942 runs batted in.

Gus' son Buddy began his major league career with the Cleveland Indians and moved on to the Texas Rangers, where he won six consecutive Gold Gloves (1979–84) at third base. His offensive numbers were comparable to his father's—a .279 average (to Gus' .281), 201 home runs (to 206), 1,106 RBIs (to 942).

Buddy's two sons, David and Mike, kept up the family tradition in the major leagues, and while they had their moments, neither had a career comparable to that of pop or grandpa.

The Alomars: In 2011 Roberto Alomar became the first son of a major leaguer to be elected to the Hall of Fame, far outdistancing the excellent careers of his father, Sandy, who batted .245, hit 13 home runs, and drove in 282 runs in 15 seasons with six teams, and his brother, Sandy Jr., who batted .273 with 112 homers and 588 RBIs in 20 seasons with seven teams. Roberto was a .300 hitter who also belted 210 home runs, drove in 1,134 runs, stole 474 bases, and set a standard on defense that few could match by winning 10 Gold Gloves in an 11-year span.

The Alous: Putting aside the unique feat that Felipe Alou was one of three brothers (the others being Matty and Jesus) who not only played in the major leagues, but on the same team and in the same outfield, it's Felipe and his son Moises who make the list. Felipe had a wonderful 17-year playing career (a .286 average, twice led the National League in hits, three All-Star selections), but his son, Moises, who also played 17 major league seasons, outdid his father. The son outhit the father by 17 points and had 2,134 hits to his dad's 2,101, 332 home runs to his dad's 206, and 1,287 RBIs to his dad's 852. But it's as a manager that father has the edge. Moises never managed in the major leagues. Felipe managed 14 seasons with the Montreal Expos and San Francisco Giants with a record of 1,033–1,021. In 1994 he brought the Expos home first in the National League East, but there was no postseason that year because of a player strike. In 2003 Alou managed the Giants to the National League West championship but was defeated by the Florida Marlins in the League Division Series.

The Fielders: Anything dad Cecil could do, son Prince could do better. Well, almost. Between them, the Fielders make up one of the greatest power-hitting father-and-son combinations in baseball history. Through 2013 the Fielders had combined to blast 604 home runs and drive in 1,878 runs...and the son had not even yet reached his prime years.

If the father could hit 50 home runs (he hit 51 in 1990), so could the son (he hit 50 in 2007, making them the only father and son to reach that milestone).

To complete the comparison, it is necessary to look at three consecutive seasons of both the father and son, the right-handed-hitting Cecil with the Detroit Tigers in 1990–1992 and the left-handed-hitting Prince with the Milwaukee Brewers in 2007–2009. Dad's power numbers for those three years were 51–132, 44–133, and 35–124, or a combined 130 homers and 389 RBIs. Son's three-year numbers were 50–119, 34–102, and 46–141, or a combined 130 home runs and 362 RBIs.

The main difference was that Cecil's three years came at ages 26, 27, and 28 and Prince's at ages 23, 24, and 25, which likely means there is much more damage to come from Prince.

The Boones: This is the first three-generation family in major league history and the only three-generation family in which all members made the All-Star team—Ray Boone, his son Bob, and his two sons, Bret and Aaron. Ray played 13 seasons in the bigs and mostly split his time equally between the Cleveland Indians and Detroit Tigers, six years each. His best years were with the Tigers. He represented them in the 1954 All-Star Game and the following year, as a Tiger, he led the American League in RBIs with 116.

Bob Boone was one of the game's most durable catchers. He wore the tools for 19 seasons, 10 with the Phillies, seven with the Angels, and two with the Royals, and made four All-Star teams. When he retired, Boone had caught 2,225 games, a major league record that was later surpassed by Carlton Fisk and Ivan Rodriguez.

Both of Bob Boone's sons, Bret and Aaron, were All-Stars. Bret had three consecutive seasons with more than 100 RBIs, including a league-leading 141 for the Seattle Mariners in 2001, 46 years after his grandfather also led the American League in RBIs. While he didn't have the career his older brother had, Aaron Boone did have one iconic moment. Playing for the Yankees in 2003, Aaron hit a dramatic game-winning, pennant-winning home run against the Boston Red Sox in the bottom of the 11th inning in Game 7 of the American League Championship Series.

The Bonds: Barry Bonds, the father, seemed headed to the Hall of Fame when injuries and a reckless lifestyle derailed a 14-year career in which he hit 332 home runs, drove in 1,024 runs, and stole 461 bases. He was the first player in major league history to record 30 home runs and 30 stolen bases in the same season more than once (he did it five times) and the second player (Willie Mays) with more than 300 home runs and 300 stolen bases in his career.

A lifetime .298 batting average for 22 seasons, a record 762 home runs, 1,996 RBIs (a staggering 1,094 home runs and 3,020 RBIs between father and son), 14 All-Star selections, seven Most

Valuable Player awards, and eight Gold Gloves would seem to make someone a no-brainer for the Baseball Hall of Fame. And yet Barry Bonds is still waiting for his call to the Hall.

My Favorite Ballparks to Hit In

1. **Riverfront Stadium:** There's no place like home, which is where the heart is and the base hits are.

2. **Dodger Stadium:** Sometimes what makes a ballpark a favorite one to hit in is not the dimensions of the outfield fences or a good hitting background. Sometimes it's the pitchers you get to face in that park. For example, many hitters will include Tiger Stadium among their favorites to hit in because it had a good hitting background and a batter could see the ball well. While that was true, it was not one of my favorites, because it meant I was going to have to hit against Jack Morris.

I include Dodger Stadium among my favorite ballparks to hit in because as great a pitching staff as they had in my time, for some reason I seemed to hit well against the Dodgers. I hit more home runs (14) against the Dodgers than against any other team. Maybe it was because when I played for the Reds, the Dodgers were our greatest rivals in the National League West and we would bear down a little harder against each other. I had pretty good luck hitting against Tommy John [Editor's Note: 25-for-58, .431], and I hit more home runs in my career off Don Sutton (6) than any other pitcher.

3. **Atlanta-Fulton County Stadium:** This was a good park for me, and for quite a few other hitters. I hit well there as a Brave and as an opponent. The ball just seemed to carry better there than in any other park. I hit 24 home runs there, the third-most in my career of any park.

4. **Yankee Stadium:** I was not a home-run hitter, but anybody who bats left-handed is a home-run threat in Yankee Stadium

because of its inviting right-field fence. I hit 32 home runs there, more than in any ballpark except Riverfront, and all of them as a Yankee. It may sound like a lot of home runs, but it wasn't. When he brought me to New York, George Steinbrenner was expecting much more. Being a left-handed hitter and with that short right-field porch, George thought he was getting a guy who could hit about 32 homers a year. I gave him his 32 home runs, but it took me four and a half seasons to get them.

5. **Fenway Park:** Right-handed hitters drool at the thought of hitting in Fenway Park and taking pot shots at that cozy Green Monster in left field that seems like it's just a pop fly away. And left-handed hitters were frustrated by the deep reaches of the fences in right field once you move a few feet off the foul line. But I was a guy who hit line drives and sprayed the ball around, and I discovered I could take the outside pitch and easily flick it to left field off that Green Monster. Let the big right-handed boppers knock themselves out trying to hit the ball over the Monster. I was satisfied to bounce the ball off the wall for singles and doubles.

[Editor's Note: Here is how Ken Griffey batted against various pitchers of his era:]

Don Sutton, 29-for-101, .287

Phil Niekro, 28-for-94, .298

*Steve Carlton, 9- for-50, .180

Nolan Ryan, 12-for-45, 10 Ks, .267

Tom Seaver, 10-for-42, .238

Rollie Fingers, 10-for-17, .588

Jim Palmer, 2-for-15, .133

Dennis Eckersley, 7-for-14, .500

Bob Gibson, 5-for-12, .417

J.R. Richard, 16-for-63, .254

Bret Saberhagen, 11-for-21, .524

Roger Clemens, 5-for-9, .556

*Bob Shirley, 8-for-46, .174, 18 Ks
*Vida Blue, 13-for-35, .371.
Burt Hooton, 7-for-39, .179
Orel Hershiser, 12-for-33, .364
*Geoff Zahn, 3-for-23, .130
*Al Hrabosky, 9-for-15, .600
*Bill Lee, 2-for-15, .133
*=Left-handed.
All statistics courtesy of BaseballReference.Com.

My Favorite Major League Cities

1. **New York:** It's the city that never sleeps and the city that has everything—Radio City, Central Park, the Empire State Building, Broadway, theaters, museums, art galleries, shops, great restaurants, all of it within walking distance of the downtown hotels where all the baseball teams stayed. When I played for the Yankees I lived in an apartment in New Jersey because what New York also has is traffic and what it does not have is ample parking.

2. **Los Angeles:** Almost as much to see and do as New York, and you can't beat the weather.

3. **Chicago:** When I played it was all day baseball in Wrigley Field, and that meant an opportunity to enjoy a good dinner with friends and family after a game.

4. **Montreal:** A beautiful city with beautiful people and old-world charm.

5. **Kansas City:** When I played for the Yankees I looked forward to road trips here because Dave Winfield and I would have an opportunity to get to Gates Barbecue at least once. Later, when I played for the Mariners, I introduced Junior to the place.

I Would Buy a Ticket To Watch....

1. **Carlos Beltran.** I like his game on offense and defense and his hustle.

2. **Albert Pujols.**

3. **Mike Trout.**

4. **Derek Jeter**, before he started to age and began breaking down.

5. **Miguel Cabrera.** I haven't seen a lot of him, but what I have seen, I admire. A great hitter from the right side. He reminds me of Edgar Martinez, who I played with in Seattle.

I also appreciate Alex Rodriguez (when he was younger) and David Ortiz. I knew Ortiz when he was just a baby, before he was Big Papi. He signed with the Seattle Mariners, but they let him go before he reached the majors. He made himself into a great hitter, especially in the clutch, and a great personality and team leader.